Working The Mum's
Guide to Childcare

The Working Mum's Guide to Childcare

SECOND EDITION

How to choose and manage the right childcare for your child

ALLISON LEE

howtobooks

Published by How To Books Ltd,
Spring Hill House, Spring Hill Road,
Begbroke, Oxford OX5 1RX, United Kingdom.
Tel: (01865) 375794. Fax: (01865) 379162.
info@howtobooks.co.uk
www.howtobooks.co.uk

How To Books greatly reduce the carbon footprint of their books by sourcing their
typesetting and printing in the UK.

First published 2008
Reprinted 2008
Second edition 2009

British Library Cataloguing in Publication Data
A catalogue record for this book is available from the British Library

ISBN: 978 1 84528 378 0

Illustrations by Phillip Burrows www.phillburrows.co.uk
Produced for How To Books by Deer Park Productions, Tavistock, Devon
Typeset by PDQ Typesetting, Newcastle-under-Lyme, Staffs.
Printed and bound by Cromwell Press Group, Trowbridge, Wiltshire

NOTE: The material contained in this book is set out in good faith for general guidance
and no liability can be accepted for loss or expense incurred as a result of relying in
particular circumstances on statements made in the book. The laws and regulations are
complex and liable to change, and readers should check the current position with the
relevant authorities before making personal arrangements.

Contents

Acknowledgements

I would like to thank Nikki Read and Giles Lewis at How to Books for giving me the opportunity of having this book published. I would also like to thank everyone on the production team who helped with the preparation and design of this book.

Finally, I would like to thank my husband Mark and sons Sam and David for being there for me, as always.

This book is dedicated to Irene Parker – with love.

Preface

It is probably true to say that childcare is one of the most stressful areas of modern parenthood. Choosing the right type of childcare and the right child carer is therefore among one of the most important decisions you will probably have to make and it is vital that you get it right.

Failing to choose wisely from the outset may result in you having to change your arrangements down the line which, in turn, can have a negative impact on your child. Ideally, with the correct information and guidance you will be able to change the mammoth, and often daunting, task of finding suitable childcare into a rewarding and enjoyable experience.

This book will attempt to equip you with the vital information needed in order for you to make an educated decision about the type of childcare you require that will meet your own individual family's needs. Just as all families are different so too are all child carers, each offering their own unique service.

Finding suitable childcare is a big decision and should not be left to the last minute. Good childcare places are often snapped up and if you don't plan early, you may well find yourself having to wait several months for a place at the nursery or childminders of your choice.

For your own peace of mind it is absolutely crucial that the childcare you choose is the right kind for you and, more importantly, your child's needs. This book is designed to help you understand the different types of childcare available and to weigh up the pros and cons of using each.

The nature of your child will have a huge impact on your choice of childcare setting and it is vital that you understand the impact that good quality childcare can have on children generally, such as encouraging confidence and independence and helping them to cooperate with each other and reach their full potential.

The differences in family structure, values and opinions make it all the more important for you to take the time to consider all the options available to you and weigh up your own circumstances, whether these be domestic, financial or work related, before coming to a decision.

What Kind of Childcare do I Require?

WHY DO PARENTS REQUIRE CHILDCARE?

There are a number of reasons why parents may choose childcare.

- They *want* to go to work.
- They *need* to go to work.
- They need space away from their children.
- They feel their children will benefit socially from mixing with a wider circle of people.

Whatever the reasons for wanting or needing childcare one thing is certain: there is a lot of choice available to parents nowadays. However, choosing the right childcare for your needs is not always as easy as it seems.

WHICH TYPE OF CHILDCARE IS BEST?

There is, of course, no straight answer to this question as the right type of childcare for you will depend on a number of factors including:

■ cost;
■ availability;
■ age of your child;
■ number of hours of childcare you require.

With a large percentage of parents returning to work after having children the decision for choosing childcare is being made by thousands of people every day. However it is important to remember that the whole process of choosing childcare is not over once you have found a provider that suits your needs. Making your choice is just the first step. You will need to prepare your child for the changes ahead, settle them into the new environment and build up a relationship with the carer you have chosen.

REGISTRATION OF CHILDCARE PROVIDERS

Registration and inspections of childcare providers are carried out by the Office for Standards in Education (Ofsted) in order to ensure that children in daycare are safe, well cared for and that their needs are met. However it is important that parents understand that not all childcare providers are registered and that even those who should, by law, be registered sometimes fail to do so.

Registered childcare providers

The types of childcare providers who require to be registered include:

- full daycare nurseries;
- sessional daycare including playgroups, pre-schools and nursery schools;
- childminders and approved home childcarers;
- crèches;
- extended schools.

Unregistered childcare providers

The types of childcare providers who do not require to be registered include:

- nannies;

- au pairs;

- babysitters;

- childminders working less than two hours per day;

- childminders who only care for children over the age of eight years. Although it is not compulsory for childminders to be registered if they only care for children aged eight years or over there are plans for the Department of Children, Schools and Families – DCSF – to introduce two registers. The register for those childminders caring for children over the age of eight years is voluntary and became fully operational in September 2008;

- relatives of the child i.e. grandparents, aunts, uncles etc.

The needs of your child

Before deciding which type of childcare *you* need it is important to first look at your *child's* needs. The key factors you should consider when choosing childcare are:

■ the age of your child;

■ the temperament of your child;

■ any worries or concerns you may have regarding your child.

THE CHILD'S AGE

As children grow and progress their needs change drastically. The childcare that you initially thought was wonderful for your tiny, helpless little baby may not appear quite as perfect when he has developed into an articulate toddler in need of stimulation and entertainment.

Continuity of care is important for the care of young children and it is therefore important, when choosing childcare initially, that you think about your child's *current* and *future* childcare needs. In order to ensure that the choice you make for your child's care when they are a baby remains suitable throughout their childhood, it is essential that you evaluate the arrangement carefully and make sure that your child will not outgrow the chosen setting.

Important needs of babies

Babies have several key needs that you must ensure your chosen carer can provide in order for your baby to be happy and settled.

Babies need:

- **Continuity of care**. This is absolutely vital. Babies need to form strong attachments to their carers in order to develop good emotional health and well being. It is important that you choose wisely at the outset as constantly changing childcare should be avoided at any age but even more so when the child is very young.

- **Affectionate, responsive carers**. Babies thrive in settings that provide them with the love and affection they crave. The carer you choose must genuinely love babies in order for your child to receive the cuddles and interaction that they need. The carer must be a responsible person who is capable of responding to your babies needs.

- **A regular routine which they know and understand**. Babies are creatures of habit and they feel safe, comfortable and secure in familiar surroundings when following a predictable routine.

- **Plenty of communication**. Although babies cannot talk they can converse through eye contact, touch and verbal noises. The carer you choose should be patient and willing to spend time with your child in this way.

- **A stimulating environment**. Babies need to be stimulated in order for them to grow and develop. A safe environment which gives them access to age-appropriate toys and equipment is vital.

Important needs of toddlers

As with babies, toddlers require:

■ continuity of care;

■ affectionate, responsive carers with plenty of patience and energy. Toddlers can be very demanding and not all carers have the stamina to deal with children of this age;

■ regular routines in familiar surroundings. Toddlers like to know what to expect and are happy when the day's routines follow a certain pattern;

■ a stimulating environment. This is essential for toddlers in order for them to be suitably entertained and to prevent them from becoming bored;

■ opportunity to converse. Toddlers ask endless questions and your child's carer will need to be patient.

Important needs of pre-school children

Once again, pre-school children require:

■ continuity of care;

■ affectionate, responsive carers;

■ a regular routine which they know and understand;

■ opportunity for conversation. The carer you choose should be aware of your child's stage of development and confident in helping and encouraging the child to listen, respond to questions and to ask questions. The carer, in return, must be responsive and be interested in and value your child's contribution;

■ a stimulating environment with toys and equipment appropriate to your child's age and stage of development.

Important needs of school-aged children

When children have started school, their needs change dramatically. They have begun to grow and mature and will be experiencing a certain amount of independence while being away from their main carers for much of the day. Although children of school age still require love, affection and continuity of care, they also need the following:

■ A quiet area to reflect on the days events, to do homework or to simply enjoy some quiet time.

■ A carer who is aware of what goes on in the school and is capable of planning their activities around the school curriculum. For example it is helpful for carers to know, in advance, what topics or themes are being studied at school as these can then be extended in the childcare setting to enhance and build on the child's knowledge. It is important of course that the carer does not repeat what has already been taught in school as this can become boring and repetitive for the child.

THE TYPES OF CHILDCARE ON OFFER

Before deciding which type of childcare you think will suit your needs the best, it is vital that you are aware of the different types available and what each has to offer. These include:

■ the childminder;
■ the nanny;
■ the nursery;
■ the extended school.

THE CHILDMINDER

There are almost 80,000 childminders in England and Wales who are responsible for the daycare of more than 300,000 children. Registered childminders are professional people who offer daycare in their own homes. The primary advantage of a childminder is that they are able to offer a 'home-from-home' environment for children and, because they operate on a much smaller scale than a nursery, they are able to give each child the individual attention they need.

Childminders are particularly successful when providing care for very young babies who have demanding feeding and sleeping patterns; as their flexible approach to childcare allows them to devote the necessary amount of time needed for children of such a young age.

Number of children registered for

Usually, childminders will be registered to care for up to three children under the age of five years with an additional three children between the ages of five and eight years. This number must include any children the childminder may have of their own. Often childminders will look after older children in addition to the younger ones as they may provide a before and after school service.

Registration requirements for childminders

In order for someone to start working as a childminder they will need to:

- be registered with Ofsted if they live in England, or the Care Standards Inspectorate for Wales (CSIW) if they live in Wales;

- be checked by the Criminal Records Bureau (CRB) to ensure that they, or anyone over the age of 16 years living on the premises where the childminding is taking place, have not been convicted of any crimes which may deem them unsuitable to be working with young children;

- have undergone a health check;

- be trained in first aid for children;

- attend introductory training;

- be familiar with the necessary criteria set out by Ofsted or CSIW;

- be insured;

- have their home inspected regularly to ensure that it is safe and suitable for young children.

In addition to the mandatory basic training, many childminders undertake additional training in order to gain childcare qualifications. They may also attend organised workshops offering advice on subjects such as nutrition, business management, child protection and behaviour management.

Although it is important that families are able to access childcare which suits their children's needs at every stage of their lives, it is also vital to remember that a vast amount of parents work shifts or unsociable hours – they may work early morning, evenings, nights, weekends or bank holidays, for example – and this is where childminders really come into their own, offering flexible hours that are often impossible to find at a nursery.

Advantages of childminders

In addition to flexibility there are many other advantages to choosing a childminder such as:

■ **Personal service**. Because childminders usually only care for a small number of children they are in the enviable position of being able to offer more individual care and attention to the children in their setting. Meeting the needs of all the children is much easier for a childminder caring for three children rather than for a nursery who may have a much larger number of children present.

■ **Consistency.** Childminders are unique in that they can offer care to a child from a young baby right through to them starting secondary school when they are usually independent young adults. This type of consistent care is beneficial to children as they are able to form a good relationship with one carer right through their childhood. The childminder and child will get to know one another very well and will, hopefully, along with the child's parents, all become firm friends. This kind of stability is essential for young children and will enable them to feel loved, valued and secure.

■ **Spontaneity**. Childminders are their own bosses and as such they decide themselves how they will spend their time during the day. They will of course need to stick to certain routines such as feeding and sleep patterns for babies and ensure that they take and collect children from playgroup

and school on time; but over and above this they do not
have a strict timetable to adhere to. This ensures ample
opportunity for important, spontaneous learning opportunities such as splashing in the puddles after a shower,
playing in the snow after a sudden flurry or making the
most of the outdoors on a sunny day. Being adaptable also
allows childminders to take their cue from the child and
should the child be feeling tired or under the weather then
suitable arrangements can be made for them.

- **Real-life opportunities**. Children who are looked after by
childminders are able to take part in everyday experiences in
much the same way as they would if they were at home with
their parents. They will be able to help with the cooking and
shopping, enjoy visits to the library or park and enjoy helping
with the gardening. These kinds of everyday activities provide
vital early learning opportunities for children with regard to
science, maths, language and social skills and enable the
children to feel part of the community. Childminders will
often attend toddler groups and support meetings along with
fellow childminders and their charges and they are able to
take and collect children from playgroup or after-school clubs,
giving the child the opportunity of making a wider circle of
friends and getting to know the area they live in.

- **Understanding**. Childminders are often mothers and
fathers themselves and as such they are aware of the
pressures faced by today's working parents. They may not
actually 'go out' to work but they are still working parents
and they will be fully aware of the demands of family life in
relation to work.

■ **Family orientated**. Unlike nurseries who often have separate rooms for children of differing ages in order to cope with larger numbers of children, childminders are able to offer care for children of varying ages, enabling siblings to stay together while they are in childcare. Most children benefit from mixing with other children of different ages and, as often the childminder's themselves will have children of their own, this may well lead to valued friendships which will stand the test of time.

> **TIP**
>
> *Before deciding on a particular childminder take the time to look around at least two others in order to get a proper 'feel' for what is on offer. How else can you be expected to make an educated decision unless you can compare different settings?*

Will a childminder be suitable for me?

To answer this question, first you will need to ask yourself:

■ Do you need flexible childcare due to irregular hours or shift patterns?

■ Do you have children of different ages whom you wish to be cared for together?

■ Do you want your child/children to be cared for by one person?

■ Do you want your child/children to be cared for in a home-based setting?

■ Are you assertive and confident in saying what you want from a childminder?

> **TIP**
>
> *When choosing a childminder, trust your instincts. The best choice for you will be someone who mirrors your parenting style and shares your values.*

THE NANNY

Nannies are employed by parents to look after their children in the family home. Nannies can either live in the family home or travel to the house on a daily basis. Nannies can be very useful for parents who work shift patterns or weekends when other types of childcare may not be available.

At present there are no legal requirements for a person applying to work as a nanny to have any qualifications, although a large percentage of nannies will have gained a recognised childcare qualification which includes:

- health and safety issues;
- physical care and development of babies and children;
- nutrition;
- understanding how children learn through play.

Types of nannies

There are six main types of nanny and these are:

- live-in nanny;
- live-out or daily nanny;
- temporary nanny;
- special needs nanny;
- nanny share;
- male nanny.

The type of nanny you will be considering will of course depend on many factors such as the age and needs of your children, your family circumstances, cost and availability.

Live-in nanny

Live-in nannies do exactly what the name suggests. They are employed by the parents to 'live in' the family home and provide childcare. Live-in nannies are usually expected to work five days per week, often from breakfast until the child's bath/bedtime in return for a salary, their own bedroom and, quite often, bathroom. You should not expect a live-in nanny to work more than 12 hours per day, however it is acceptable to arrange separate evening babysitting cover. This extra cover should be arranged with the nanny and is often one or two nights per week. Nannies usually expect two full days off each week.

Live-out/daily nanny

A live-out or daily nanny is employed for a certain number of hours per day during which time they come to the family home. Once again hours should be negotiated but should not exceed ten hours per day with additional babysitting in the evening if necessary. Live-out or daily nannies are usually only required during the time that the child's parents are working and therefore may often finish work earlier than a live-in nanny who may be expected to bath the children and get them ready for bed.

As a live-out or daily nanny is not provided with accommodation, their salaries are usually much higher than a live-in nanny whose salary will reflect the fact that they do not have to pay for their own living expenses.

Temporary nanny

Temporary nannies provide parents with short-term or emergency childcare and can be useful at times when the family's usual nanny is ill or on holiday or if the family has been let down unexpectedly. Temporary nanny contracts can last anything from a few days to several months depending on the circumstances and they may be employed either on a live-in or live-out basis. Temporary nannies often demand higher rates of pay.

Special needs nanny

There may be times when a child who is suffering from a special illness or condition will require specialist care. Obviously the severity of the child's condition will go a long way to deciding whether additional care is required. Special needs nannies are particularly good at caring for children suffering from profound or multiple physical, sensory or mental disabilities.

In order for some children with special needs to reach their full potential it is sometimes necessary for them to receive specialist care from an experienced person who is highly trained in areas such as sign language, Makaton, or chronic illnesses. This is where a special needs nanny may be able to provide the solution.

TIP

There are no legal requirements for a person applying to work as a nanny to have any childcare or first aid qualifications. It is essential, therefore, if you are considering this type of childcare, that you ensure that the person you choose to care for your child is suitable and that they have the necessary skills required for such a demanding and responsible role. Ask for references and, more importantly, follow these up!

Nanny share

A nanny share provides a more economical way for parents to employ the services of a trained nanny. A nanny share can be particularly useful for families who have children of school age or for parents who work on a part-time basis. The latter scenario might see a nanny working three days per week with one family and the remainder with another. Nanny shares usually work on a live-out or daily basis.

A nanny share may also work well for parents who work full time and the nanny is employed to look after the children of two families, in the home of one of them, sharing the costs involved.

Male nanny

Very few workers in the childcare industry, and this includes nursery workers, childminders, nannies and extended schools, are male. This is probably because, in the past, childcare has always been seen as women's work. However things are now beginning to change and more and more men are entering the world of childminding and nannying.

Male nannies can be particularly beneficial to working single mothers who are worried that their children do not have regular contact with a male role model.

It has been reported in the press that male nannies are also becoming popular with working women who often see female nannies as a threat to their marriage.

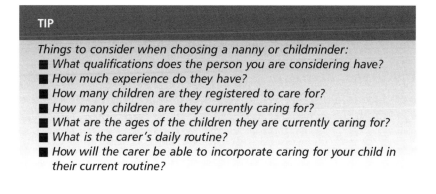

Things to consider when choosing a nanny or childminder:
- *What qualifications does the person you are considering have?*
- *How much experience do they have?*
- *How many children are they registered to care for?*
- *How many children are they currently caring for?*
- *What are the ages of the children they are currently caring for?*
- *What is the carer's daily routine?*
- *How will the carer be able to incorporate caring for your child in their current routine?*

Will a nanny be suitable for me?

To answer this question, first you will need to ask yourself:

- Do you prefer someone to care for your child in your own home?

- Do you have children of varying ages and wish for them to be cared for together?

- Are you prepared for someone to live and/or work in your home?

- Do you need someone who can fit around your routine?

- Do you wish to have a lot of input in the way your children are cared for?

- Are you willing to take on the legal and financial responsibilities that employing a nanny entails?

THE NURSERY

Nurseries usually offer childcare to children aged between three months and five years old and are less flexible when it comes to opening hours compared to some other forms of childcare. Often a nursery will operate from 8am to 6pm, which can be a problem for parents working shifts or weekends.

Unlike with nannies or childminders, children who are being cared for in a nursery will often have contact with several carers on a daily basis which may make it more difficult for them to 'bond' with one special person. Often this problem can be resolved by using a key person system, whereby a parent and child are allocated a key member of the nursery staff who becomes the main point of contact for the parent with regard to the child's progress and development. This member of staff will be responsible for building a relationship with your child.

Ofsted are responsible for the registering and monitoring of children's nurseries and strict regulations must be adhered to.

Types of nursery

There are three main types of nursery and these are:

- private nurseries;
- workplace nurseries;
- council nurseries.

Private nurseries

Private nurseries are readily available in most areas. These nurseries charge a fee for the care of the children and many offer 'specialist' services such as webcams to enable parents to access the internet in order to see their child during the day. Some may offer foreign language tuition, dancing classes, or provide organic food on their menus.

Workplace nurseries

This type of nursery is primarily for companies who reserve places for the children of their employees. Often if the nursery has any vacancies these will be offered to non-employees.

Council nurseries

Run by local councils, these nurseries are free but are very difficult to get into. Places in council nurseries are usually reserved for children from families in special circumstances such as one-parent families.

Advantages of nurseries

One of the main advantages of a nursery is the reliability that they offer. Nurseries are usually open all year round with the exception of Christmas and New Year. Parents can therefore always be sure that childcare will be available and they do not run the risk of their nanny or childminder letting them down at the last minute due to illness, nor do they have to organise holiday cover.

Disadvantages of nurseries

One of the main disadvantages of using a nursery is their lack of flexibility. Parents will be expected to collect their children on time every day and often, premium rates are charged for late collections. This is quite simply because staff are paid for a set number of working hours and expect to finish at their contracted time. Insurance complications may also arise if the nursery has to stay open longer than its core operating hours.

Although nurseries enable children to mix with a number of other adults and children and can give children confidence for being away from their parents, which can be especially useful when the child is almost at school age, nurseries can also be rather daunting for a shy child who may find the whole experience of spending time in a nursery setting overwhelming.

> **TIP**
>
> *Take your cue from your child. There may be a nursery within a stone's throw from your front door offering a service for up to 60 children. However, if your child is shy and reserved by nature, is this really the best environment to put them in while you go to work? Sometimes compromises have to be made and travelling to a smaller nursery isn't much of a price to pay if your child is happy and settled in a more compact setting.*

Will a nursery be suitable for me?

To answer this question, first you will need to ask yourself:

- Do you prefer your child/children to be cared for by more than one person?

- Do you find it difficult to arrange sick and holiday cover and therefore need a setting which offers year round care?

- Do you want your child/children to mix with plenty of other children?

- Do your working hours fit around the opening hours of most nurseries?

- Is your child ready for new experiences?

- Is your child sociable and confident enough to mix with a large number of people?

THE EXTENDED SCHOOL

Many schools have recognised the needs of working parents and as such have opened their doors to allow children to spend longer hours in school thus enabling parents to drop their children off earlier and collect them later.

Breakfast clubs

Breakfast clubs usually open between 7.45am and the start of the school day and offer school-age children breakfast and a safe environment to stay before school commences for lessons.

After school clubs

Extensions to the core school hours see children also being offered tea, activities and a quiet place to do their homework and many schools now stay open until 6pm.

Advantages of extended schools

These early starts and late evenings have been recognised as helping a large number of working parents by providing them with somewhere for their child to stay outside of the school's usual working day. Although not all schools currently offer this service, the government announced, in its ten-year childcare strategy in December 2004, that it intended to enable all primary schools to become 'extended schools' in England or 'community focused schools' in Wales by 2010. This would mean that the schools targeted would offer childcare to the local community from 8am until 6pm each day, including school holidays.

Disadvantages of extended schools

Some people will argue that our schools are a place for learning and should not be offering a 'babysitting' service to working parents. They believe that it is not good for a child to be spending up to ten hours per day in school, having breakfast, lunch and tea there. Others, however, argue that extended schools help working parents enormously and that they are the answer to many parents' childcare needs, particularly parents who prefer to leave their child in one familiar setting rather then transferring them to a childminder.

> **TIP**
>
> *Bear in mind that not all schools offer extended hours and those that do may only be available in term time. If you choose this type of childcare you will need to think about making separate arrangements for the school holidays.*

Will an extended school be suitable for me?

To answer this question, first you will need to ask yourself:

- Is it easier for you to drop off and collect your child from one place each day?

- Do you prefer your child to stay in the school environment they know well?

- Do the opening hours of an extended school successfully bridge the gap between school hours and your working hours?

■ Do you have cover for the school holidays? Often extended schools are only available during term time, leaving a gap in childcare of around 13 weeks per annum.

THE PROS AND CONS OF THE DIFFERENT TYPES OF CHILDCARE

There are both advantages and disadvantages with every type of childcare and it is important that you consider all the implications carefully before choosing which type of childcare to go for. If, after asking yourself the questions posed above, you are still a little unsure then consider the following summary of pros and cons for childcare both in your own home i.e. a nanny or au pair; or outside the home i.e. a day nursery or childminder.

Childcare in the home: nanny, home child carer, au pair, mother's help

Advantages

■ You will not be required to travel to take your child to and collect them from a different location.

■ There will be little disruption to your child's daily routine. For example, they will not have to be woken early to get ready in order to be at the childminder's or nursery on time. Often a nanny will arrive at the family home while the children are still asleep. This type of arrangement is particularly useful if the child is feeling a little under the weather or has had a late or troubled night.

■ Siblings can be cared for together.

- Children are often much more confident when in familiar surroundings and this can be particularly useful if you have a very shy child who finds it difficult to mix.

- The care given by a home-based carer is much more personal and can be tailored to your child's specific needs.

- You will have the opportunity to have much more say in the way your child is being cared for.

- If you work from home you will have contact with your child whenever you wish.

- The care provided is much less formal than in a day nursery.

Disadvantages

- Many child carers who work in the child's own home are unregistered and hold no qualifications, i.e. au pairs and mother's helps, and may need supervision.

- There is a lot of work involved in hiring a carer, such as a nanny, and you will be responsible for being their boss, giving instructions and paying their tax and National Insurance contributions.

- You may be left without cover when the carer is ill or on holiday.

- Nannies and other carers who work in your home can be an expensive choice as they may incur additional household expenses (if they live in), insurance and travel expenses, not to mention agency fees if you have used an agency to help you find the right person.

- There is the loss of privacy to consider if you employ a live-in nanny.

- Children often get much closer to one carer who works closely with them and, if the carer leaves, it can affect your child emotionally.

- Parents may become jealous and envious of the close relationship their child has with their carer.

Childcare outside the home: childminder, day nursery, playgroup, out-of-school care

Advantages

- A system of government checks are in place to ensure that children have access to high quality childcare and an early years curriculum.

- Staff are trained and the premises will have undergone rigorous checks to ensure safety.

- They are reliable and, in the case of nurseries, will have cover in place for staff holidays and sickness.

- The care is readily available most of the year. Many nurseries and childminders offer care for between 48 and 52 weeks of the year.

- Your child will enjoy a wide range of toys, equipment and activities that are planned and appropriate to their age and stage of development.

- Children are eased into the formal care, which prepares them for school.

- Children can spend time with other children of a similar age.

- You get valuable time and space away from your child.

- This type of childcare is one of the cheapest forms around, particularly if you take advantage of the free childcare places for three-and four-year-olds or if you work for an employer who offers you the chance of joining a childcare voucher scheme. (There is more information about childcare vouchers in Chapter 9 of this book.)

Disadvantages

- You will need to take and collect your child from the setting.

- You may not have as much input into your child's daily care as you may like.

- Your child may spend many hours each day away from their home environment.

- Your child may not be able to spend the day with their siblings if being cared for in a nursery, as many have separate baby and toddler rooms.

- It is common for the turnover of staff in a nursery to be quite high making it more difficult for a child to bond with one particular person.

- You will need to organise cover for when your child is ill as they will be unable to attend a childminding or nursery setting. Likewise if your childminder is ill, you will need to organise alternative childcare cover.

■ Your child may find it difficult to mix with larger groups of children in a nursery setting particularly if they are shy by nature.

■ You may not always agree with the settings policies or the way in which certain situations are handled.

❝ I have experience of working with children as young as three years of age who attend several childcare settings in one day. It is possible for a young child to attend a childminding setting from 7.30am before being taken to pre-school at 9.00am, followed by a lunch club and then being taken to a state nursery until 3.30pm, after which they are collected by the childminder and cared for until 6.00pm when their parent finishes work.

Although this can, and does, work well for some children it does need careful consideration. The child is effectively spending their time in four different settings in the space of approximately 10 hours and this can be daunting for a lot of children. Often settling three- to four-year-olds into one setting can be challenging, therefore expecting them to settle into four settings may be asking just a little too much! ❞

2

Preparing Yourself

KNOW YOUR RIGHTS

The Government reviewed its maternity policy for mothers whose babies were due on or after 1 April 2007. All mothers-to-be are now entitled to six months Ordinary Maternity Leave (OML) together with six months Additional Maternity Leave (AML) regardless of how long they have been working in their existing job. If you are intending to return to work before the end of the full year you will need to give your employer eight weeks' notice of your intention to go back to work.

If you have worked for your current employer for at least 26 weeks by the end of the 15th week before the beginning of the week when your baby is due, and you have been earning at least £90 a week before tax, you will be entitled to Statutory Maternity

Pay (SMP). If you qualify, this means you will be entitled to 90 per cent of your usual wages for the first six weeks followed by either 90 per cent of your usual weekly wages or £117.18 per week (whichever is the lower) for the remaining 33 weeks.

Partners of new mothers are also entitled to two weeks' paternity leave if they have worked for the same employer for at least 26 weeks by the end of the 15th week before the beginning of the week when the baby is due. Most men who are entitled to paternity leave are also eligible for Statutory Paternity Pay (SPP). SPP is either 90 per cent of the father's usual earnings or £117.18 per week once again, whichever is the lower.

The introduction of 'keeping in touch' days has now made it possible for women who are on maternity leave and claiming SMP to work for a maximum of ten days without having to sacrifice their SMP, as they have had to do in the past.

RETURNING TO WORK OR STUDY

Once your maternity leave has finished you are entitled to return to the same, or similar, job you had before the birth of your baby. The job must carry the same, or better, terms and conditions as previously. The only exception to this rule is if you have been made redundant. If you don't go back to work after your maternity leave has come to an end you will not be required to repay any SMP you have received, however, if your employer has paid you additional maternity pay on top of your SMP, you may be required to repay this if you decide not to return to work under the agreed terms.

There are both practical and emotional issues involved in

holding down a job, running a home and being a good parent. Every parent wants the best for their child but sometimes, in order for us to achieve this, we feel we are fighting a losing battle. All parents, at some time, will have feelings of inadequacy and wonder if they are doing the right thing. It is perfectly natural to have these feelings and, in order to have the best of both worlds – an enjoyable, rewarding career and a happy, stable home life – it will be necessary for you to prepare yourself for the transition of returning to work or study. Finding the right childcare for your needs is, of course, one of the most important factors of easing yourself successfully back into the workplace and this book will help you to do just that. However, there are a number of other issues you will need to deal with in order to enable you to be sure the commitment you have made is one you can confidently keep.

Preparing yourself

- Talk to your employers or college. Let them know your situation and try to negotiate arrangements that will suit everyone.

- Make sure that your employers are aware that you may, from time to time, need to take emergency leave at short notice. This is an unavoidable part of all working parents' lives and you should not feel embarrassed or make excuses for the odd 'blip' in childcare cover.

- Enquire about help with childcare costs. There is more on financial assistance in Chapter 9.

- Plan your day. Take pressure off yourself by establishing routines and making diary notes to prevent you from forgetting important dates and events.

■ Delegate. Get your partner or, if you have any, older children to shoulder some of the responsibilities of running the house. Don't allow yourself to become a martyr.

■ Don't push for perfection. Ease up on yourself, no one is going to notice if you don't polish the furniture every day or clean the windows every week.

Getting back into the working routine

Most of us are a little apprehensive about returning to work after having a couple of weeks off for a holiday so, returning after several months of maternity leave can be very daunting. There are several ways in which you can make the transition easier for yourself:

■ Be strict from the start. By making sure you leave on time, every day you will be able to spend more time with your baby once you are at home. It is all too easy to fall into the trap of working late. If you start by doing this a couple of nights a week you may quickly find yourself working more and more late nights until your time spent at work is much more than that spent at home, upsetting the family–work balance.

■ Ensure you have a back up plan in place in case you are caught in traffic or miss the last bus/train. This will ensure you do not panic if you find yourself running late and unable to collect your child on time from the nursery or childminder.

■ Make time for your work colleagues. It probably won't be

easy for you to socialise with colleagues after work, as you may once have done before having a family, but there is nothing preventing you from catching up with them during your lunch hour, so make the most of this time.

■ Focus on the benefits. Instead of looking at the negative side of things concentrate on the positive things. Your child will benefit from mixing with other children and enjoy the time they spend at a nursery or childminder and the financial rewards of going back to work will benefit the whole family.

BALANCING WORK AND FAMILY LIFE

Your time at home with your children is precious and never more so than when you return to work. Your job may be very important to you and you may have worked very hard in the years before starting a family, building up a successful career. Understandably, you want this career back and the rewards that come with it. However it is important that you remember that your life changes dramatically when you become a parent and your career, though important, can not be allowed to take over your life as it may once have done.

Working 15-hour days at the office will no longer be an option – even with the most understanding childminder – and let's face it, do the rewards really amount to that much? Are you prepared to miss out on your baby just to climb a few rungs of the career ladder? I hope your answer to this question is no and it is my guess, if you are reading this book, that you are as eager to balance your work and family life as you are to making the best choice in childcare.

> **TIP**
>
> *Balancing family and work life and making the best possible choice in childcare go hand in hand. A successful family life needs parental input and this can only be achieved if the parents spend quality time with their children.*

Working parents' choices

As a working parent you have a number of choices and rights which will enable it to be easier for you to combine work and family life. For a start, you will be entitled to certain benefits when you are pregnant and when you become a new parent, and these benefits will enable you to take paid time off to attend antenatal appointments. New mums are entitled to paid maternity leave to enable them to spend time after the birth at home with their child.

FLEXIBLE WORKING HOURS

Working parents have numerous rights. For instance you have the right to request flexible work options such as term-time work or to take part in a jobshare scheme, both of which are designed to make combining work and family life easier. Parents of children under the age of six years can apply for flexible working hours, including the option of working from home, once they have been working for their employer for six months. Since this law came into effect, over a million parents have taken advantage of flexible working hours.

In order to make a request to work flexible hours you will need to complete a form which is available by logging on to www.dti.gov.uk/workingparents. Your boss may, of course, refuse your request for flexible working hours but to do this they will need to provide you with a clear business reason for their refusal, in writing.

Different types of working hours

There are a number of different patterns you may like to consider with regard to working hours.

- **Part time**. This consists of an employee working less than the regular number of hours worked in a week. Your rights must remain the same as any other employee regardless of whether they work longer hours than you or not.

- **Job sharing**. This is when a job is split between two employees. All income, pension and benefit rights are also divided.

- **Flexi-working**. This is when an employee agrees to work set core hours for example between 10am and 2pm. Outside of these core hours you are allowed to dip in and out as you like, enabling you to clock up a fixed amount of time.

- **Term-time hours**. This is when parents are allowed to work during school term time only taking unpaid leave during school holidays. Salary payments are usually spread over 12 months enabling you to receive the same amount of money in wages each week or month.

- **School hours**. This enables parents with children of school age to be able to drop their children off and collect them from school each day. Employees working school hours are usually expected to work during school holidays, therefore you will need to make arrangements for childcare during these times.

- **Compressed hours**. This is when employees are allowed to work longer hours but over fewer days. For example, instead of working eight hours per day, five days per week you may be able to work ten hours per day for four days per week.

- **Staggered hours**. This is when employees are allowed to start work earlier and finish earlier or start later and finish later. This kind of working day may suit parents who work shift patterns. For example one parent may work 6am–2pm while the other works 3pm–11pm.

- **Home working**. This is when employees are allowed to carry out their work from home. You may be expected to go into the office for meetings when required.

All of these working patterns have been designed to make employment a more suitable option for parents and should help to address the issue of balancing work and family life.

It is important, when looking at your work options, that you do not appear difficult or make unreasonable demands on your employer. Try to see things from everyone's perspective – not just your own – in order to find the best possible solution for everyone.

3

The Search Begins

WHERE DO I START LOOKING FOR CHILDCARE?

The answer to this question depends very much on the type of childcare you are looking for. Hopefully, after reading Chapter 1, you will be in a position to distinguish between the different types of childcare available and you should by now have decided which type of childcare you feel would best suit your needs.

It may be that, although you have decided on a home-based child carer, you are undecided as to whether you would like to employ the services of a childminder or a nanny and you may continue to feel this way until you have looked at the facilities that both have to offer and perhaps even interviewed several possible candidates. This type of 'open mindedness' is to be welcomed and encouraged. By taking your time at the beginning of your search for suitable childcare, you stand a much better chance of finding the right person for the job rather than blindly jumping in and leaving a lot to fate.

As a childminder myself, I always encourage potential customers to look at other settings before making their mind up. This is not because I am trying to lose customers. On the contrary, I fully believe that by encouraging parents to see everything that is on offer, when they do decide on suitable childcare, the chances are that they will be happy with their choice and the start of a long-term relationship will begin. I may risk losing the prospective customer to a 'rival' childminder but I console myself with the fact that the parents will be happy with the choice they have made and hopefully, so too will the children.

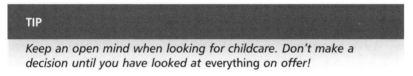

TIP

Keep an open mind when looking for childcare. Don't make a decision until you have looked at everything on offer!

So, you have now got some idea of the *type* of person you would like to place the responsibility of the care of your child with. The next big step is finding your ideal childminder, nanny or nursery. If you have older children who are at school and you have decided on enrolling them in the breakfast and after school club the chances are that this will be at the school that you have already chosen to send your child to and you will therefore be happy with the setting and facilities.

The childminder

There are a number of ways in which to source a suitable childminder.

- **Children's Information Service (CIS)**. Contact your local CIS for details of childminders in your area. Information such as the fees charged and the schools serviced may also be included in the details, which will go a long way to helping you to decide whether the service being offered suits your needs prior to making an appointment.

- To find out the contact details of your nearest CIS visit the Childcare Link website on www.childcarelink.gov.uk or telephone freephone 0800 096 0296.

- **Word of mouth**. Ask your friends and work colleagues, who have children, who they use and enquire about vacancies there. Personal recommendation is one of the best ways of securing a good childminder. Making enquiries may help you to secure a place that is due to become vacant but has not yet been advertised.

- **Advertisements**. Look at the notice boards in your local schools, library, doctors and dentists surgeries as these are often places where childminders place adverts if they have any vacancies.

- **National Childminding Association (NCMA)**. The NCMA has been working with Care-4, one of Britain's largest providers of childcare vouchers, to develop Childcare Places – a brand new website to help childminders fill their childcare vacancies and to enable working parents to access suitable childcare. Parents who work for some of the UK's leading employers such as BT, Tesco and John Lewis and who have access to Care-4 childcare vouchers can visit www.child careplaces.co.uk for details of childminders advertising their vacancies. The site is password protected to allow access to

NCMA members and Care-4 parents only so you can be sure to source childcare places safely and securely.

- **Yellow Pages**. Some childminders may offer their services in the *Yellow Pages* or *Thomson Local Directory*. Details can be found under the section headed *childminders and crèches.*

The nanny

There are many places you can look for the services of a nanny, including nanny recruitment agencies, advertisements in local newspapers or specialist magazines, the internet and even childcare colleges.

- **Nanny recruitment agencies**. These types of agencies can be located by looking in the *Yellow Pages* or in specialist magazines such as *Nursery World* or *The Lady*. Agencies may also be sourced over the internet.

- **Word of mouth**. As with childminders, a recommendation for a good nanny or nanny agency from a friend or colleague who has used one successfully, can be very helpful.

- **Advertisements**. Many nannies advertise their services in local newspapers, on the internet or on the notice boards of local doctors, children's clinics etc. Advertisements in specialist magazines such as *The Lady* should also be considered.

- **Childcare colleges**. Consider placing an advertisement on the notice board of your local colleges offering childcare classes to attract the attention of students who are coming towards the end of their training and will be looking for suitable employment.

> **TIP**
>
> *If searching through the advertisements does not bring any luck try placing your own advert expressing your wish to employ a nanny. Keep your advert short and to the point giving details of the hours required and the ages of the children to be cared for. It is advisable to use a box number for replies to your advert rather than giving your personal contact details, to avoid unwanted attention.*

Nurseries

It is relatively easy to find a nursery as they are usually located in busy areas, many of which you may drive past during your daily commute to work. Nurseries, unlike childminders and nannies, have the added benefit of having signs advertising their service outside the premises and usually have a marketing budget for placing adverts in local newspapers and distributing flyers advertising their service. Nurseries can also be sourced through the following.

- **Children's Information Service (CIS)**. Visit your nearest branch, look on the website www.childcarelink.gov.uk or telephone freephone 0800 096 0296.

- **Advertisements**. Check adverts in your local newspaper for vacancies. Large promotional advertisements are often placed in local newspapers periodically.

- *Yellow Pages*. Many nurseries have their contact details listed in the *Yellow Pages* under the section headed *day nurseries*.

- **Word of mouth**. As with all childcare, let your colleagues, friends and family know that you are looking for a suitable nursery and ask whether they can recommend anyone who may have a vacancy.

Points to consider

When visiting childcare settings consider the following:

- Are the staff trained and experienced?
- Is the atmosphere relaxed?
- Are the children happy and suitably entertained?
- Are the premises safe and clean?
- Are there sufficient planned activities suitable for the age and stage of development of your own particular child?
- Are the staff welcoming?
- Do *you* like the setting?
- Would *your* child like the setting?

Extended schools

As mentioned previously, the extended school you choose will probably be part of the same school your children are already attending during the day as transportation problems will arise if you select a different school. However, it is important to remember that not all schools offer extended hours at present and this may be something you will need to consider when choosing which school you intend to enrol your child at.

If the services of an extended school are vital to you then make sure you opt to send your child to a school which provides this service in order to avoid disappointment at a later date. It is also worth bearing in mind that the extended school will not be run by the same members of staff who teach your child during the school day, therefore it is essential that you meet the staff and ensure that you are happy with the facilities and activities on offer.

WHEN SHOULD I START LOOKING FOR CHILDCARE?

You can never start your search for suitable childcare too early. Having said that, a common sense approach should be used. Don't start telephoning potential childminders, nannies and nurseries saying that you are hoping to become pregnant in the next two to three years and could you book a place now – you won't be allowed to!

However it is possible, and indeed it is necessary, to plan ahead with regard to childcare. If you are expecting your first child and planning to return to work after the birth, use your maternity leave to source suitable childcare. This will give you ample time to choose the right type of childcare, at a time before the baby has been born and when you are probably relaxed, without the added task of caring for a new baby. If you find suitable childcare while you are pregnant you will be able to use your maternity leave to build up a friendship with the childminder or nanny you are wishing to employ or, if you have chosen a nursery, you will be able to visit on several occasions to get to know the staff. All this is vital in order to put your mind at rest and help you to feel completely sure that you have chosen the right childcare for your family's needs.

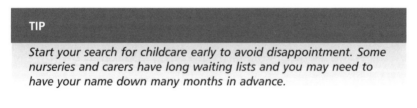

TIP

Start your search for childcare early to avoid disappointment. Some nurseries and carers have long waiting lists and you may need to have your name down many months in advance.

If you are looking for alternative childcare, for example, if your child is currently being cared for at a nursery and you will need to change your childcare arrangements when your child starts school, then you should have a date in mind when this transition will take place.

You should be looking several months in advance in order to secure suitable childcare and introduce your child to his or her new carer. For example, if your child is due to start school in September it is not too early to start looking for a childminder or extended school in April. This will enable you to arrange for your child to visit their new surroundings prior to the often daunting task of starting school, in order that they have eased themselves into the new childcare arrangements before the school term begins.

An added benefit of planning ahead and sourcing childcare several months in advance is that you will be in a good position to secure a place as soon as it becomes available, if an immediate vacancy can not be reserved.

TIP

Always remember that places with a good childminder, nanny or nursery are often difficult to secure and, when vacancies do arise, they seldom stay that way for long!

Of course, not everyone will be in a position to spend three or four months sourcing childcare at a leisurely pace. You may find yourself in the unenviable position of being let down by your existing provider resulting in you having very little time to make alternative arrangements. *Never* feel pressured into leaving your child with someone whom you feel is unsuitable, even for the short term.

It is not a good idea to swap childcare arrangements often as you risk unsettling your child's routine and threaten to upset their security. If necessary, book a week or two holiday entitlement to allow yourself the time to source suitable childcare in order to ensure that the person you are leaving your child with is someone suitable rather then simply someone who is available and convenient!

> ❛*Allowing yourself sufficient time to source suitable childcare is a must. I have had parents telephone me on a Friday requesting a place for their child to begin the following Monday. Leaving things to the last minute like this is asking for trouble. Even if a place was available at such short notice, which is highly unlikely, you will not have left any time to discuss arrangements, sign contracts, get to know the setting and the staff or settle your child in. I would not be happy giving up my well-earned weekend to settle a child into my setting and discuss childcare if the parent couldn't be bothered to spend some of her maternity leave doing the kind of research which is vital when sourcing childcare.*❜

FACTORS INFLUENCING PARENTS' DECISIONS

Armed with the knowledge of where to look for childcare and when to start looking you should be well on the way to having a good idea as to which type of childcare you are hoping to secure. However, evaluating the pros and cons of each type of childcare provision is not always easy. A lot will depend on your child, your income and the area in which you live.

You will need to consider the following factors before making a final decision.

- The age and social ability of your child.
- Your working hours.

- The level of care you require – whether your child has any special requirements.
- The availability of your preferred childcare.
- Whether you have had any recommendations.
- Cost.
- Government initiatives – whether you can claim any help towards your childcare costs, often this can only be accessed if you put your child in *registered* childcare such as with a childminder or in a nursery. Nannies are not presently registered.
- Shift patterns.
- School terms.

Visiting settings

Once you have drawn up a shortlist of preferred carers you will need to make arrangements to visit the providers to look over their premises and discuss your requirements. Give yourself plenty of time and do not try to cram in too many visits in a short space of time. If possible, take your child along with you and either your partner or a friend so that you can both get a 'feel' for the environment and talk things through together.

The setting's atmosphere

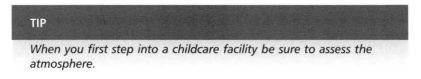

TIP

When you first step into a childcare facility be sure to assess the atmosphere.

All the toys and equipment money can buy will be of little benefit to the children if the general atmosphere of the setting is unwelcoming and negative. Children need positive, happy environments in order for them to thrive and enjoy their time in the setting. Staff should be polite and helpful and, above all else, approachable. Look at the way the staff or provider mixes with the children, do they listen to what the children have to say, answer their questions and value their opinions?

It is ultimately the staff who dictate the tone of the setting and its success. If they are positive, well motivated and enjoy the job that they do then this will come across in the way they interact with the children. Pleasant, patient providers will encourage the children in the setting to build on their confidence and self-esteem and the atmosphere of the setting will have the necessary 'feel-good' factor.

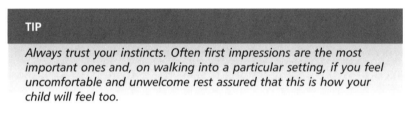

TIP

Always trust your instincts. Often first impressions are the most important ones and, on walking into a particular setting, if you feel uncomfortable and unwelcome rest assured that this is how your child will feel too.

CHECKING FACILITIES

When visiting settings, there are a number of things which you should be looking at and checking in order to reassure yourself that the care on offer is suitable for your and your child's needs. You should be checking:

- the indoor area and facilities;
- the outdoor area and facilities;
- the routines on offer;
- the activities on offer.

The indoor area and facilities

This is the first area of the setting that you will really notice and, as such, it is probably true to say that the provider has spent a lot of time and resources making this area the best that they can. If the room is dull and shabby and the toys worn and broken you can rest assured that the rest of the provision will not be up to scratch either. In addition to being safe and inviting the indoor area should be child-friendly and appealing. It should be clean, bright and colourful.

The indoor area should provide adequate areas to play, eat, sleep and rest and the facilities provided should be sufficient for all ages and stages of development of the children being cared for.

The indoor facilities should provide opportunities for imaginative and creative play, together with resources to provide learning opportunities. Toys, games and books should be in good, clean condition and, once again, appropriate to the age and stage of development of the children being cared for.

As part of my own research into childcare, I have made appointments to look around daycare settings and found some of them to be seriously lacking. After contacting nurseries I have found on occasion that information is scarce and appointments to look around are not encouraged. As a parent I would view this as highly suspicious.

One of the nurseries I did look around did nothing to ease my doubt. It was drab, dirty and soulless. An unpleasant odour encompassed the building and the sight of a dirty nappy left in a potty did nothing to ease my mind with regard to health, hygiene and the cleanliness of the staff working there. These are the kinds of things you should be looking out for when you visit any setting.

At the other end of the spectrum I have looked at childminding and nursery settings which are bright, clean and welcoming, with an array of suitable toys and equipment. The staff were genuinely warm and helpful and I know, given the choice, which setting I would choose for my own child. Looking at different settings is absolutely essential before making any decisions.

The outdoor area and facilities

If the indoor area and facilities meets with your approval, next turn your attention to the outdoor area. Is this safe and secure? Are the children prevented from accessing dangers such as drains, greenhouses and ponds? Does the carer have adequate outdoor equipment such as ride-on toys, a sand pit, climbing frames etc? Look out for other imaginative play equipment such as small apparatus for use with obstacle courses, for example hoops, cones and balancing beams, a Wendy house or 'den' and perhaps facilities for planting and growing fruit, vegetables and flowers and for studying nature.

In addition to making sure that the carer provides sufficient indoor and outdoor toys and equipment and a welcoming and inviting atmosphere, it will be necessary for you to use your visit to reassure yourself of the other important aspects of your child's care such as:

■ Safety – what are the settings regulations with regard to fire precautions, collection of children, treatment of accidents etc?

- Smoking – does the setting have a no-smoking policy in place which is strictly enforced?

- Does the setting have any pets and, if so, what access do the children have to them?

- Are the premises clean?

- Personal hygiene – do the children and staff present look clean? It is important that providers encourage good personal hygiene.

- Look at the toilets – are they clean and easily accessible to the children?

- Hand-washing facilities – do the children have access to suitable hand-washing facilities with hot and cold water, soap and paper towels?

- Look at the kitchen/food preparation areas – are these clean and hygienic?

The routines on offer

Ask the staff or provider about the daily routines and reassure yourself that these comply with the way you would like your child to be cared for. There is more about routines in Chapter 6.

The activities on offer

Ask about the activities the setting offers and enquire which specific activities or learning experiences will be particularly suited to your child's age and stage of development. Does the setting offer regular outings or visits to libraries and museums for example? There is more information about activities in Chapter 5.

The general atmosphere of the setting

As I have mentioned previously, the general atmosphere of the setting is crucial for the well being of the children present. The children should be interested and absorbed in the activities on offer and you should check carefully to make sure that their needs are being catered for. Children who have insufficient activities and resources to keep them entertained and amused will quickly become bored and disruptive.

The staff and whether they appear friendly and approachable

If the children appear largely to be fending for themselves with little or no interaction from the provider or staff then this is a cause for concern. It shows that staff are uninterested in the children and that the children have learned not to request help. Staff should participate in activities and know when to give assistance and when to allow the child to try to work things out for themselves. They should *always* be on hand to praise and encourage the child.

As well as setting a good example when working with the children, the staff should also:

- offer support and encouragement to the children when they are playing;

- talk to children at their own level. They should get down to the child's height and talk to them in a manner appropriate to their age and level of understanding;

- be kind, patient and affectionate;

- offer reassurance if a child is upset or hurt;

■ be genuinely interested in the children and what they have to say;

■ offer praise and encouragement;

■ be at ease with the children;

■ be alert and aware of the things going on around them.

Staff should appear to work together as a team, share ideas and get along together in order for things to run smoothly and to create a positive atmosphere. Children will quickly sense any animosity between members of staff and pick up on conflict, which may well result in the child becoming anxious in the company of certain staff members. Try to speak to as many members of staff as possible in order to get a feel for their ideas and opinions and, if possible, talk to parents of children already attending the setting. Ask to look at the settings latest inspection report, which may well comment on the way staff work together as a team. Staff who work well together will:

■ be happy in each other's company;
■ encourage and reassure one another;
■ be on hand to help each other;
■ converse with others pleasantly and positively.

INTERVIEWING CARERS

Where and when the interview takes place will depend very much on the type of childcare provider you have decided on. If you like the idea of your child being cared for by a childminder then you will have to telephone the childminder to make a mutual appointment to visit them in their own home; likewise a nursery setting will require you to visit the premises at a convenient time and date. If you have decided to employ a nanny then they will obviously need to come to your home for an interview.

Prior to any interview:

- telephone initially to book a suitable date and time;

- read any CVs you may have;

- follow up any references you have been given;

- obtain a copy of the provider's latest inspection report, if they have one, and read it thoroughly;

- make appointments to see several providers so that you have something to compare each with;

- make a list of questions you would like to ask.

When the interview takes place, try to be as confident as possible without dictating or demanding. Although it is essential to be honest and explain exactly what kind of childcare you had envisaged for your child you should also bear in mind that it may be necessary for you to compromise in some areas, particularly if you are intending using the services of a provider who may have several children on their books.

Don't be blasé about things. You have a very important decision to make and, as such, should treat the interview with the importance it deserves. If you do not understand something the provider has told you or you are in any doubt whatsoever about any aspect of the childcare on offer, then ask. Clearing up any misunderstandings at this stage may save you a lot of hassle in the long run.

> **TIP**
>
> *Don't feel pressurised into signing anything at the initial interview stage – even if you are being badgered by an over-zealous provider touting for business. They may tell you that places rarely remain available for long and you risk losing the place if you don't sign immediately; however it is important that you allow yourself the time to mull over the interview and think about the facilities on offer and, if at all possible, look at other settings for a comparison.*

HOW DO I KNOW IF I HAVE FOUND THE RIGHT CHILDCARE?

The answer to this question is quite simply – you don't! You should do your research and look at as many settings as possible in order to get a 'feel' for different types of childcare so that, when you have made your decision, you can be as certain as possible that your decision is the right one. However, it is not usually until the placement has begun when you can be really *sure* whether you have found the right childcare or whether you have made a big mistake!

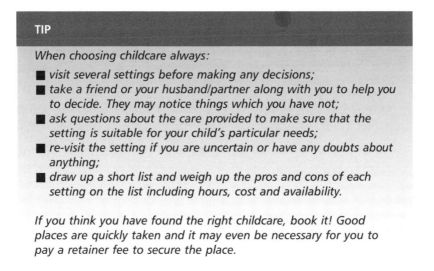

> **TIP**
>
> *When choosing childcare always:*
> - *visit several settings before making any decisions;*
> - *take a friend or your husband/partner along with you to help you to decide. They may notice things which you have not;*
> - *ask questions about the care provided to make sure that the setting is suitable for your child's particular needs;*
> - *re-visit the setting if you are uncertain or have any doubts about anything;*
> - *draw up a short list and weigh up the pros and cons of each setting on the list including hours, cost and availability.*
>
> *If you think you have found the right childcare, book it! Good places are quickly taken and it may even be necessary for you to pay a retainer fee to secure the place.*

Interviews, though useful initially, are usually used by the prospective childminder, nanny or nursery as a chance to 'sell' themselves. You can therefore be faced with an eager person who is trying very hard to secure your business; promising everything you need and leaving you thinking that you won't be able to live your life without them.

Reputable childcarers should not promise you anything they can not deliver but, unfortunately this is not always the case and some childcarers are desperate to secure business at whatever price. Although in theory this may sound good to you, the parent, finding someone who will bend over backwards to accommodate your every wish may sound very tempting. Don't be fooled, as this kind of person rarely exists and a childcarer promising you the earth will either quickly tire of your demands or change the arrangements agreed at the first opportunity.

Key factors to help minimise mistakes when choosing childcare

Although there is no foolproof way of ensuring that you never make a mistake when choosing childcare, there are some key factors you should bear in mind to minimise any potential mistakes.

✓ Look at as many settings as possible before making your decision. If you are not sure about whether to look at childminders or nurseries then look at them both before making your mind up.

✓ Make a list of the pros and cons for each type of childcare and weigh up both.

✓ Don't exclude any type of childcare simply because of the cost. There may be ways around the potential expense of a nanny, for example if you consider a 'nanny share'.

✓ Be honest with yourself! If you don't want your child to become attached to one person then a childminder or nanny may not be for you. On the other hand, if you are unhappy with your baby being cared for by several members of staff then a nursery may not suit your needs.

✓ When you do interview childminders and nannies or look around nurseries, tell them *exactly* what you are looking for and allow them to decide whether they can accommodate your wishes. If you find it difficult to get to the nursery before 6.15pm and they close at 6pm then you are asking for trouble. Explain your dilemma and, if the nursery is not willing or is unable to extend their hours then you will have to look elsewhere for childcare. This does not mean that your child can't attend *any* nursery; it simply means that you may have to find one nearer to your workplace in order to be able to collect your child on time or find one that has longer opening hours.

In contrast, childminders will probably be more flexible with their hours providing you are honest with them from the start. There is nothing more frustrating for anyone than not knowing when their working day will end, particularly if the childminder has a family and commitments of their own. Resentment will grow if you say one thing but, when the contract commences, mean something very different.

✓ Consider the costs. Are the prices being charged excessively high or worryingly low? A high fee does not necessarily mean a high quality of service. Low fees, though tempting, may signal a desperate struggle for business where a childcare provider has to resort to undercutting their rivals to secure customers, rather than depending on the strength of their service. Find out what the asking price includes. A low fee may not seem quite as attractive when you add on items such as meals, nappies and toiletries, if these are not already included. Higher fees may in fact be a better proposition if all these essentials are included and may even work out cheaper in the long run.

✓ Look at the children already present in the setting. Do they seem happy, sociable and entertained? Are there sufficient staff to meet the required adult:staff ratios? Childminders are usually allowed to care for three children under the age of five years. Of these three children not more than one may be under the age of 12 months. Childminders may also care for older, school-age children providing that the total number of children does not exceed six under the age of eight years. These numbers *must* include any children of their own.

✓ In nurseries, one adult is usually allowed to care for three children between the ages of three months to two years. For two- to three-year-olds, it is one adult to four children and for three- to seven-year-olds, this ratio increases to one adult for every eight children.

✓ Enquire about the facilities on offer. In the case of a childminder, who will have a limited supply of toys and equipment compared to a large nursery, ensure that they have the toys and facilities suitable for the age and stage of development of *your* child.

✓ Enquire about any regular planned outings. Childminders often introduce the children in their care to the community by visiting local libraries, toddler groups, playgroups etc. Check that the provider you are considering has an itinerary suitable for the age of your child.

✓ Enquire about the settings' policies and procedures concerning safety, equal opportunities, behaviour, confidentiality and illness.

✓ Ask to see the qualifications held by the staff. Although there is no compulsory training for nannies most will be NNEB trained. Childminders must attend basic training and many then choose to develop their training and complete the Diploma in Home-based Childcare or take a National Vocational Qualification (NVQ) in childcare. Many childcare practitioners also show commitment to their jobs by undergoing Quality Assurance training, which shows prospective customers that the practice has been checked and monitored to provide quality childcare. Staff employed by a nursery should hold suitable qualifications depending on the age of the children they are looking after. All childminders and nannies must be trained in paediatric first aid, likewise sufficient members of staff working within a nursery setting should also hold a first aid qualification.

If you take your time and look at *all* the available types of childcare on offer before making up your mind, you will stand a better chance of making the right decision and finding a suitable person to care for your child. However, it is not always possible to find the right person at the first attempt and, even the most methodical parents who have interviewed dozens of potential carers, can end up with an unsuitable childminder, nanny or nursery.

Although ideally a child will not be subjected to too many disruptions, and any changes in childcare should be kept to a minimum, it is possible to correct any mistakes without upsetting the child's routine too much. If you have made a mistake it is best to own up and admit it to yourself and then set about making amends than to shrug it off in the hope that things will improve with time. It is probably true to say that your child is the most precious thing in your life and as such you should leave nothing to fate when it comes to finding a suitable person to care for them when you can't be there yourself.

Making it Work

THE RELATIONSHIP BETWEEN THE PARENT AND THE CARER

The relationship you have with your child's carer is crucial to the success of any business arrangement. It is likely that, in the case of a childminder or nanny, it will be the individual's personality as much as their qualifications and experience that attracted you to them in the first place.

The relationship you strike up with your child's carer is very important and it will mean the difference between you forging a good, stable friendship which will benefit everyone involved, or a distant acquaintance which is of much less benefit, particularly to your child. Often childminders and nannies in particular, become very good friends with the families they work with and these friendships can last for years. Ideally this is the kind of relationship to work towards as the rewards are high and your child will benefit from becoming part of such a close-knit family arrangement.

Friendships may be much harder to build within a nursery environment because of the number of staff involved and the potential for the turnover of staff to be greater; however it is possible to build a good relationship with one or two 'key' workers who will get to know your child well and this is something you should be aiming for and building on.

Unannounced visits to the setting

A good nursery or childcare provider will operate an 'open door' policy whereby they are happy for parents to drop in unannounced to discuss any aspects of their child's care or any concerns or worries they may have. However some nurseries may discourage unplanned visits and prefer you to make an appointment to discuss any issues.

Although I would be wary if a nursery openly discouraged any kind of unannounced visits it should also be recognised that these requests are often made for a reason. Parents turning up unannounced can upset the daily routine of the nursery, unsettle the children and even distract the staff.

Nurseries and other providers who welcome parental help should be looked at favourably. Although you yourself may not have the time to commit to a regular session helping out at your child's nursery, it is always a good sign if parents are encouraged to actively take part in their child's care in this way. For one thing, welcoming parents into the setting, shows that the provider has nothing to hide!

Positive signs to look for from the carer

You can be confident that the relationship you have with your child's carer is a good one if:

- the carer shows the same kind of values towards children as you do;

- the carer welcomes you into the setting and is friendly, open and honest;

- the carer is helpful and genuinely interested in you, your child and your family;

- the carer is professional;

- the carer has taken the time to get to know your child well and can talk to you about their needs, their likes and their dislikes;

- the carer shows a keen interest and real pride in their work;

- you feel confident that you can talk to your child's carer about any issues or concerns you may have and that you will be taken seriously and listened to.

Signs for concern

You should be concerned if:

- your child's carer often looks stressed and tired;
- you feel unable to approach the carer with any issues or concerns;
- you feel that your child is not being cared for properly;
- your child is unhappy;
- you do not feel welcome in the setting;

- you are undermined and made to feel uneasy if you raise any questions or concerns;
- other parents using the service are unhappy.

When everything is taken into account it is important to remember that for any business arrangement to be successful, both parties must respect each other's opinions and individuality. Constructive criticism should always be seen in a positive light however, negative opinions and unjustified remarks should be avoided at all costs.

> **TIP**
>
> *Just as you have a right to civility, so too does the carer you have chosen for your child. Respect has to be earned and cannot be demanded.*

Working in partnership with the childcare provider

The single most important thing for parents and carers to remember is that they should be *working in partnership* with one another at all times while caring for the child. You, the parents, are the most important people in your child's life. You will know your child better than anyone else and you have the right to request that your child is cared for in a way that is acceptable to you.

By employing the services of a childminder, nanny or nursery you are not handing over the reins of parenting and allowing the carer to do as they see fit, you are trusting them to care for your child in a way that you have *requested* and you have the right to expect your wishes to be respected.

Other children

Although you are the child's parent it is also important to remember that you will probably not be the only family who has put their trust in the carer you yourself have chosen, unless you have employed a nanny solely to care for your child in your own home. If you take your child to a nursery you must remember that your child may be one of perhaps 30 other children and there will need to be some element of compromise in order for every child, from every family, to be accommodated successfully.

Childminders will be working in their own home, often caring for children from several families, and as such they may have certain rules that, although you may not always agree with, you may have to abide by in order to ensure a good relationship. For example a childminder may have three children along with their parents arriving at their home every day and if they request that you remove outdoor shoes before trudging over the lounge carpet you should be prepared to do so, even if it is not something you yourself would expect in your own home.

Respect your child's carer and they will respect you. Trust will grow when the partnership you have with your chosen child carer is working well and likewise your chosen carer will feel valued and respected. A harmonious working relationship is beneficial for everyone concerned.

Parents need to show practitioners that they have their backing on issues such as behaviour. Children will be happy and secure when they know the boundaries and there may be times when the parent needs to back up the carer to show the child just who is the boss.

I have had children in my own setting who, for the majority of the time, are kind, considerate and generally very well behaved. However, as soon as a parent arrives to collect them they take this as their cue to abuse my property, run riot and answer back. When parents are not present the children know the rules and are aware of what is and is not acceptable. It is, however, a very grey area for children when a parent arrives, as they think they will be allowed to do as they please because no one will tell them off.

Parents need to know that this kind of behaviour will not be tolerated and it is important that children are chastised if they are doing something which is against the usual rules. As a parent, how would you feel if half a dozen children used your sofa as a trampoline or crayoned on the walls of your living room?

Points to bear in mind

In order to develop a positive working relationship with your child's carer it is important to:

- communicate openly and effectively;

- be honest;

- show sensitivity and compassion;

- work cooperatively together and seek constructive solutions to any problems which may arise;

- be as flexible as possible;

- be willing to compromise if necessary;

- keep your part of the contract and ensure that you collect your child on time, pay on time and provide your childminder, nanny or nursery with the necessary provisions they have requested in order for them to carry out their duties successfully.

■ have a positive attitude.

THE RELATIONSHIP BETWEEN THE CHILD AND THE CARER

There has always been the suspicion, whether this is unfounded or not, that a child being left with a nanny or childminder may grow increasingly attached to their carer and could even end up becoming closer to them than to their actual parents. Many parents returning to work dismiss the idea of a one-to-one carer for their child purely for this reason, opting instead for a larger nursery setting where their child is less likely to form an intimate bond with a member of staff.

Putting your mind at rest

This kind of problem is not insurmountable and, with open communication about feelings and worries, the carer could easily put your mind at rest. Most nannies and childminders will tell you that they are not trying to be surrogate mothers to the children in their care and many will go out of their way to reassure you that they respect your relationship with your child and never try to compete with or undermine your authority. If you do have these kinds of fears, which are perfectly reasonable, explain them to your chosen carer so that you can work together to find a solution.

I am a childminder myself. I am also a mother. Although I care greatly for the children in my care I have never wished to take the place of their parents and my feelings towards these children are very different from those I have for my own two sons. I completely respect and value the opinions of all of the parents and the children I look after and I genuinely believe this is one of the most important factors of a successful working relationship.

A nanny is in the enviable position of being able to encourage the parents to spend more time with their children by helping out with essential household chores such as preparing the child's meals or washing and ironing the child's clothes. By carrying out these chores themselves it leaves the parent with extra time to devote to their offspring.

Becoming attached

Putting competition for affection aside for now, let us think closely about the relationship between the child and their carer. Should we be fearful of a close bond in case this threatens to upset the relationship the child has with their parents? Should we be pleased if our child appears to idolise his/her new carer? Should we encourage the relationship to blossom? Although all of these questions need careful consideration it is probably true to say that most parents will be happy if they know that their child enjoys spending time with their carer.

The key to finding the right childcare is not just to find someone who provides the right service, which is available for the necessary hours and charges a reasonable rate. More importantly the right childcare setting is a place where your child can feel happy, loved and valued. A place where they enjoy playing and learning and somewhere they look forward to going each day.

Surely it is more important to ignore your pangs of doubt over the loving relationship your child has with his or her carer and be grateful that you have found someone your child obviously enjoys being with rather than for you to go to work each day with a nagging doubt in the back of your mind that you are worried your child is unhappy? There is nothing more heart wrenching for a parent than for them to leave a sobbing child behind while they rush off to work.

When your child is unhappy

Although some mothers return to work because they enjoy their job and simply do not wish to give up their careers to stay at home seven days a week, it is also the case that other parents go to work because finances dictate that they have to. Whether you are a slave to your mortgage or a career-minded business woman, leaving a child with tears rolling down their face in an environment where they are not happy would melt even the hardest of hearts. That is not to say that every child who cries after mum is not happy two minutes after their mother has climbed into the car and driven off. Many children cry when being left and this is not the kind of 'upset' you should be concerned about. No one knows your child like you do and it is up to you to talk to your child and more importantly *listen* to what they have to say.

TIP

*Remember to work **with** your child's carer and do not see them as someone competing against you for your child's affection. A competent childminder, nanny or nursery nurse will be sensitive to your feelings and will make sure that they do everything possible to reassure you that you will always be the most important person in your child's life.*

PARENT OR CARER – WHO IS THE BOSS?

This is always a difficult question to answer and, depending on who is doing the answering, the outcome may be very different! The carer would almost certainly answer that, when on *their* premises the *carer* is the boss and the parent will argue that as they are responsible for their child then they are *always* the boss.

Perhaps then the most sensible way of looking at this question would be to ask whether it is actually necessary to have a 'boss' at all. Is there really any need for the parent to be in charge of the carer or vice versa? Undoubtedly the parent has the final say in what type of care they require for their child, and the wishes of the parent must be considered at all times. However, surely the best way of achieving good quality childcare is to work in *partnership* with each other as a team eliminating the need for either the parent or the carer to have the upper hand.

PARENTS AND CARERS – WORKING IN PARTNERSHIP

As parents, you are the first educators of your children. When choosing suitable childcare for your children you will have taken into account many things before coming to a final decision. When you do decide whether to employ the services of a childminder or nanny or whether you choose to leave your child in a nursery, your decision will have been made mainly by preference and what you yourself believe to be the most suitable choice for your child.

Your choice of childcare will reflect the types of things you consider to be important with regard to the welfare of your child. You will have looked around the setting and interviewed or spoken with various people offering childcare services, however it is what happens *after* you have made your decision which really counts. Never let yourself believe that the hard work has been done just because you have decided on which childminder or nursery to send your child to or which nanny will be arriving every morning to take over the childcare duties. Finding the right carer is only the start of the journey and *working* at making the relationship work is the real achievement.

> **TIP**
>
> *Ways to get the best out of your child's carer:*
> - **Employ the right person!** *Follow the guidance given in this book and take your time. Make sure that the person you choose enjoys the job and is happy with the arrangements involved.*
> - **Communicate well**. *To get the best from your child's carer it is vital that you communicate well at all times.*
> - **Show your appreciation**. *We all work well with praise. Let your carer know if you are pleased with the service they provide and they are more likely to consistently give their best. People who feel that they are being taken for granted or are unappreciated quickly lose interest and become bored.*
> - **Be friendly and approachable**. *Just as it is important that you are made to feel that you can discuss any issues with the carer, so too must the carer feel they can approach you with any issues or concerns they may have.*
> - **Be assertive**. *If your carer is doing something you are unhappy with then tell them. Do not dither; say what you mean but do so respectfully. If the carer makes a genuine mistake accept their apology and let it go. It is of no benefit to anyone to keep on dragging up past mistakes or making the carer feel inadequate or humiliated.*

DEVELOPING RELATIONSHIPS

There are two main aspects of developing relationships and these are:

- exchanging information;
- maintaining communication.

Exchanging information

Without good – and reciprocal – communication it will be impossible for you to build a good relationship with your child's carer.

It is absolutely vital that you, the parents, exchange information with the person or persons you have trusted with your child's daycare. There is little point in having certain ideas of how you would like things to be done and what you expect from your childminder/nanny/nursery if you fall short of sharing your ideas and views with them. Childcarers, though often competent, bright and very capable people, lack mind reading skills and even they need a little guidance when it comes to understanding exactly what you expect of them!

Exchanging information between parents and carers is something that should be done on a regular basis and, ideally a few minutes every day should be set aside to discuss your child's daily routine. It is not always easy to make time to do this as both you and your child's carer will be tired and busy at the end of the day. However, it is very important both for your child's continuity of care and for your own professional relationship with your chosen carer, to ensure that a daily exchange of information does take place.

Many childminders and nurseries issue the children in their care with a journal, which can be used as a way for both parents and carers to note down information that they feel the other needs to know about. Then, if anything crops up which needs to be discussed in detail, an appointment can be arranged at a time which is convenient for everyone.

> **TIP**
>
> *Always remember that the role of your child's carer is to complement yours as a parent. Never try to compete with your chosen carer, work together to build up a positive relationship which will benefit your child.*

Why you need to exchange information with your child's carer

Exchanging information with your child's carer is paramount in order for you both to be happy and confident that the child is receiving the best possible care and to ensure the continuity of that care. As parents you need to know that your wishes are being respected and childcarers need to be certain that they are fulfilling their duties adequately. The only real way either party can be completely certain that the child being cared for is happy is by *communicating and exchanging information.*

How to communicate effectively with your child's carer

- Take the opportunity when you drop off and collect your child to exchange important information such as sleep and eating patterns. If your child has had a bad night it is important that you inform the carer so that they can keep an eye open for any signs of imminent illness or so that they are aware that your child may be more tired than usual.

- Request appointments periodically to discuss your child's progress and use these appointments to bring any concerns or issues you may have to the carer's attention.

■ Make sure that you are aware of all the policies and procedures which the setting has in place (you should be furnished with a copy of each).

■ Familiarise yourself with the setting's daily routines.

■ Read notice boards and newsletters to keep up to date of events and special dates.

■ Make sure that you regularly update the information your carer holds for your child, such as contact numbers.

■ Ask to see the records and progress accounts the setting holds for your child.

■ Take an interest in what your child does with their carer. Be aware of the topics and themes being studied and take the time to look at the work your child has done which may be displayed on the walls of the setting.

■ Make sure you are aware of your obligations and that you fulfil them.

■ If you have any questions about anything concerning your child's care then ASK!

The kind of information you and your child's carer need to exchange

In addition to needing to know that your child is happy, you may also like to be made aware of a number of other things that your child has been doing during their time with the childminder or nanny or while they have attended nursery. Try not to be too demanding of your carer's time by expecting them to log, word for word, every single conversation they have had with your child throughout the day or exactly how many carrots they ate at lunchtime. The important information you and your child's carer should be exchanging includes the following:

- **A brief outline of your child's day**. Ask what kind or activities your child has taken part in and which they particularly enjoyed.

- **Meals and snacks**. Ask about the menu. This information should satisfy you that the children are being given a well balanced, nutritious diet and will outline any concerns, for example if they have eaten very little this could be a sign of a lack of appetite due to feeling unwell.

- **Toilet and nappy routines**. A child who is feeling unwell may show signs in a number of ways, one being a lack of appetite and another being through their toilet or nappy routines. Too few or too many visits to the toilet or dirty nappies could be a sign of illness or constipation, both of which will need to be addressed.

- **Rest and sleep patterns**. These are particularly important for babies and young children and discussing your child's sleep patterns will help both you and your child's carer to understand your child's needs regarding rest periods for the day.

- **Behaviour**. Any child who behaves in a way that is out of context should be monitored. It is vital that both you and your child's carer should be aware of any changes to your child's behaviour and, if the behaviour gives cause for concern, you will need to discuss what needs to be done together.

■ **Causes for concern**. There may be times when your child has become upset either at home or while with their carer and any incidents such as these should be shared so that all the adults are aware if the child has needed to be comforted and reassured for any reason during the day.

Maintaining communication

In order for you to communicate effectively with your child's carer or nursery it is absolutely vital that you are:

■ honest;
■ open;
■ friendly;
■ approachable.

Always remember that your child's welfare depends very much on the information you give to your child's carer and false or inaccurate information will be of benefit to no one. Although everyone has their own opinions and ideas, it is important to remember that these will vary between families and just as you have the right to have your values respected so too have other people – including the carer themselves. Never speak to your child's carer disrespectfully as this will achieve nothing. If you have something to say about the service you are receiving then do so in a calm, relaxed and friendly manner if you hope to achieve a positive outcome.

You should feel that your childminder, nanny or nursery nurse is someone you can turn to for practical help and advice and who can offer you support should you need it.

Although remaining on friendly terms with the person you have chosen to care for your child should be of paramount importance to you, it is also important that you remember to keep a balance between your friendship and the business side of things. Just because you and your childminder are 'friends' does not mean that either of you should feel that you are being taken for granted nor should unacceptable compromises have to be made by either party.

TIP

There is a difference between 'being friendly' and 'becoming friends'. Although it is vital for everyone to be friendly you must decide just how friendly you wish to become with your child's carer. Parents who put their children in the care of a nursery will rarely have this type of problem simply because of the number of staff employed in a nursery; however parents who employ the services of a childminder or nanny may well find themselves in the position of becoming very good friends with their child's carer. This is fine if both parties are happy with the arrangement and, in many cases childminders and nannies become firm friends of the family throughout the whole of the child's lives. However, problems may arise if parents feel that the service they are paying for is bring compromised because of the friendship or if they have difficulty being professional for fear or upsetting a 'friend'.

Staying involved

The secret to successful childcare is for you to stay involved and to continue maintaining and developing a good relationship with your child's carer. Never fall into the trap of thinking that because you have found childcare that you are happy with that your job is done and you can forget about the whole thing. As I have mentioned before *finding* the right childcare is the easy part. Maintaining a happy relationship requires time and effort from everyone and is essential.

To promote good working relations make sure you review your child's needs regularly. As your child grows and develops their needs will inevitably change. Look at how you can work with your child's carer in order to adapt to take into account your child's changing needs.

FEELINGS OF GUILT

Parents who are looking for childcare often approach the task with a wealth of complex feelings. Even if you have found a childminder, nanny or nursery to leave your child with that you are 100 per cent satisfied with and have no worries whatsoever about the way they will care for your child, you may still experience a whole range of other feelings, some of which you never thought you would, such as:

- sadness leaving your child behind;
- anxiety about whether you are doing the right thing;
- jealousy because of your child's feelings for the carer;
- guilt because you enjoy your job.

First and foremost it is important that you realise that *all* of these feelings are perfectly natural and most parents will experience one or all of them at some point when they return to work. You *will* think about your child while you are at work and, more importantly, you *should* think about your child while you are at work. However, it is better that your feelings are constructive rather than negative in order for you both to enjoy and benefit from your time apart.

Continuity of care

As I have mentioned previously, your child will thrive if there is continuity of care between yourself and the person you trust with their childcare and it is therefore paramount that you put your feelings of doubt and guilt to one side if the whole situation of you returning to work is going to be a successful one. If you are going to spend all your time looking for or even creating problems then your return to work is doubtless set to fail. However if you see the situation in a positive light and do your best to work in partnership with your chosen carer, casting aside any unfounded feelings of guilt and jealousy, then there is absolutely no reason whatsoever why you can't enjoy job satisfaction safe in the knowledge that your child is having fun and being well cared for by the person of your choice.

> **TIP**
>
> *Look at your child's carer as an equal. Respect the job they do and keep any feelings of jealousy or resentment you may feel from time to time to yourself. Surely it is better that your child spends their time away from you with someone they love and enjoy being with rather than being unhappy so that you don't feel pushed out?*

5

What Will My Child be Doing When in Childcare?

WHAT DO YOU WANT FOR YOUR CHILD?

The way your child will spend their days while in daycare will depend very much on the type of daycare you choose for them. The experiences they enjoy at a childminder for example will be very different from those provided by a day nursery and you should think carefully about how you would like your child to spend their time before making your final decision on childcare.

As mentioned in Chapter 1, childminders provide 'home-based' childcare which will often reflect the kind of things your child will probably be doing when they are at home with you. A nanny will provide daycare in your own home and therefore your child's environment will remain the same and only their carer will be different. A nursery, on the other hand, will offer a much more structured daily routine which will have little in common with your home setting.

Pros and cons

It is not really appropriate to discuss here which option is best, as each of us will have our own ideas and opinions on this which is why all the pros and cons should be looked at for each type of daycare before a decision is made. Some people may argue that childminders and nannies are better suited to the care of very young babies as they can devote the time needed for such a demanding routine of feeds, sleeps and nappy changes without having a lot of other children to care for. Others will argue that, once a child reaches two or three years of age they are ready to move out of the home environment into a more structured learning environment. I would say that all this is a matter of opinion and much will depend on the nature of your child and indeed your own preferences to childcare.

What I would stress to you, however, is that you make yourself aware of what each provider has to offer and be confident that this is what you want. There is little point for example enrolling your child in a large, 50-place nursery if you want them to take part in the usual everyday activities you enjoy together such as shopping, making the tea, sorting the washing and snuggling up on the sofa after lunch for an hour every day – this simply will not happen in a nursery!

In much the same way, although many childminders and nannies are competent in providing early years education for your child, they may have limited resources compared to a large nursery which may provide computers, interactive white-boards, a large outdoor playground and other expensive items of equipment that their large budgets may allow.

EDUCATION, EDUCATION, EDUCATION

What is the right age for a child to begin learning? The answer to this question is quite simply: from birth! In fact it may well be argued that babies begin learning from the moment of conception when they learn to recognise sounds from inside the womb. From the minute a baby is born they begin to become aware of their surroundings and to use their senses. With the correct stimulation the child will continue to learn and develop.

It is important for you to make enquiries about the learning opportunities your child is likely to receive while in daycare in order to satisfy yourself that this is the kind of early education you require for your child.

Learning opportunities likely to be provided by childminders

Many childminders base their learning opportunities around the everyday situations available in the home. The majority of parents who choose a childminder to care for their child do so because of the 'home-from-home' environment they have to offer.

Children being cared for by a childminder will often get the opportunity to become a real part of the family and will enjoy associated experiences. These may including the following.

- **Cooking and baking**. Childminders have the opportunity of being able to allow the children in their care the chance to help to prepare and cook meals. Childminders often bake buns and cakes with the children.

- **Shopping**. Although it is not appropriate for childminders to conduct a marathon monthly shopping spree while caring for children, many learning opportunities can be enjoyed when enjoying a trip to the bakery or greengrocers. Children can be encouraged to choose their favourite fruits and given the opportunity to pay for the goods themselves. Shopping for birthday cards and gifts is also a good way of helping the children to integrate into their local community and learn about shopping for others.

- **Setting the table and clearing away**. Although not many people will understand how invaluable this kind of activity is for children, it has to be said that early numeracy and communication skills are developed when carrying out simple tasks like these. Talking to the children about what they are doing is essential to their language development and encouraging the child to count how many people will be eating and then work out how many pieces of cutlery will be needed is a fun way of introducing early maths.

- **Sorting clean washing**. This is another excellent way of encouraging children to become involved in early numeracy. For instance, getting children to sort socks into colours and pairs introduces early mathematical skills.

Childminders are very adept at using the opportunities and resources available within the home to encourage early education. In addition to the above everyday experiences, childminders should also have a good selection of books, games and resources available which are appropriate to the age and stage of development of all of the children they are caring for. You would be well advised to ensure that this is the case before putting your child in their care. A good childminder will show you the materials and resources they provide and explain how they encourage and support early learning. Childminders should also provide opportunities for the children in their care to:

- paint;
- colour and draw;
- cut out and glue;
- enjoy junk modelling;
- enjoy jigsaws and other puzzles;
- take part in games;
- enjoy construction;
- role play and dressing up;
- make music;
- enjoy dance;
- enjoy stories and books;
- take part in spontaneous play;
- mix with other children by attending local support groups and toddler groups;
- enjoy trips to local parks, playgrounds and museums. Indoor play gyms sometimes offer discounted rates for childminders and the children they care for and many childminders take advantage of these offers.

Learning opportunities likely to be provided by nannies

It is probably true to say that the toys and resources your child will enjoy while being cared for by a nanny will be down to you as the parent, as your child will be cared for in their own home with their own toys and equipment. You should discuss with your nanny what kind of learning resources and equipment he or she considers appropriate and either you will be expected to provide these or you should fund the purchases your nanny makes. As with the children being cared for by a childminder, those whose care is being provided by a nanny will have the benefit of taking part in all of the everyday experiences such as shopping and cooking and becoming a part of the local community.

The nanny you choose should be creative and resourceful. They will need to have the ability to stimulate your child's imagination in addition to knowing how to provide games and activities which will encourage their overall development.

Remember that although nannies do expect to have to do some household chores such as cooking, shopping and washing and ironing the child's clothes, it is important, if you want your nanny to interact mainly with your child, that you do not expect her to carry out too many household chores. If you expect your nanny to wash and iron for an hour a day and then go shopping for another two hours, this is three hours of her time which she is not devoting to your child.

TIP

You need to limit the number of hours your nanny will spend cleaning and ensure that she spends much of her time with your child doing the job she is actually qualified to do.

Learning opportunities likely to be provided by nurseries

Nursery settings are much more likely to provide *structured* activities and learning opportunities are more likely to be planned. Although time should always be available for children to play spontaneously and for them to choose their own toys or activities, nurseries will also offer many planned activities designed to promote children's early education.

Children in a large nursery setting will have the opportunity to mix with others of a similar age and will be encouraged to take part in a wide range of activities. Children from all walks of life, with different backgrounds and from different cultures will all spend time together and this is a good way of encouraging children to enjoy the diversity of the country we live in today.

Although it is probably harder for children in a nursery setting to become a part of their own immediate community, as many children attend nurseries near to their parents' workplace rather than in their home area, they will still experience trips to local playgrounds, museums etc. Nurseries will usually provide the following activities and experiences for children in their care:

- painting;
- drawing and crayoning;
- sand and water play;
- dressing up and role play;
- computer activities;
- junk modelling and collage making;
- games and puzzles;
- music and dance.

THE LEARNING PROCESS

In previous years, providers of childcare for infants and toddlers in England were expected to follow the Birth to Three Matters framework. Activities in nurseries, playgroups and childminding settings are based on four areas of development. These areas are:

1. A strong child.
2. A skilful communicator.
3. A competent learner.
4. A healthy child.

From September 2008, the Birth to Three Matters framework (outlined above) was replaced by the Early Years Foundation Stage (EYFS). The EYFS is a single framework for care, learning and development for children in all early years settings from birth to the August after their fifth birthday. The EYFS builds on the existing Curriculum Guidance for the Foundation Stage, the Birth to Three Matters framework and the National Standards for Under 8s Day Care and Childminding.

The aim of the EYFS

The main aim of the EYFS is to help young children achieve the five *Every Child Matters* outcomes. These outcomes are as follows:

- staying safe;
- being healthy;
- enjoying and achieving;
- making a positive contribution;
- achieving economic well being.

The principles of the EYFS guide the work of all practitioners and are grouped into four distinct themes:

1. A unique child.
2. Positive relationships.
3. Enabling environments.
4. Learning and development.

Areas of learning and development

The principles, pedagogy and practice from Birth to Three Matters have been retained and each of the following areas of learning and development reflect the existing 'stepping stones' approach to the Foundation Stage:

- personal, social and emotional development;
- communication, language and literacy;
- problem solving, reasoning and numeracy;
- knowledge and understanding of the world;
- physical development;
- creative development.

It is important therefore that the provider you chose to care for your child is aware of both the Birth to Three Matters Framework and its replacement the Early Years Foundation Stage and that they are confident in applying these strategies to their daily work.

PLAYING OR LEARNING?

When does a child stop playing and begin to learn? When does a child give learning a rest to enjoy playing? Many adults seem to want to differentiate between playing and learning and often find it difficult to understand which of the two is the most important for the child's development. Well, the truth of the matter is that playing is learning! Children who enjoy taking part in games and activities while playing are also learning.

Children are learning *all* the time whether they are taking part in a game of snap or baking a cake for tea. Everything a child does is a learning experience for them. Whether they enjoy their learning experiences and wish to repeat them is largely down to the adults. Adults who make learning fun and enjoyable are much more likely to stimulate the children in their care and encourage them to want to learn. Hurried, unimaginative activities will often end up leaving the child uninspired and disillusioned having learned little if anything, and the child will not be in a rush to repeat the experience.

Building children's confidence

Children need to be encouraged to take part in suitable activities in order to promote their learning and development and they need to be happy and confident when carrying out certain tasks. Children need to feel competent and, with the help and encouragement of the adults around them, they will have the confidence to try out new tasks and experiment which is essential in order for them to achieve their full potential.

Suitable adults

Whatever type of childcare you decide on for your child, either home based or nursery based, you will need to be sure that the adults you are trusting with the care of your child are both experienced and qualified in early years' care. Your child needs to spend their time in a stimulating environment with adults who are both eager and willing to encourage them to learn and develop. Your child will need to be encouraged to develop:

- language and communication skills;
- intellectual skills;
- literacy skills;
- numeracy skills.

The adults trusted with your child's care will need to be confident and competent and know how to encourage children to grow and develop in these areas.

Language and communication skills

- Your chosen nanny, childminder or nursery nurse will need to know how to communicate with your child on *every* level. Children ask endless questions and your child's carer will need to demonstrate patience and be willing to talk about everything!

- Children need to take part in activities in order to learn and they should be encouraged to join in and to talk about what they are doing, seeing and experiencing.

- Listen to the way your child's carer communicates with your child. Do they speak slowly and precisely using words which your child finds easy to understand or do they mumble, speak too quickly and use complicated language which your child has difficulty understanding? Although it is important that adults do not over simplify language or use 'baby talk' they should make sure that they speak slowly and clearly in order to be understood. Repetition is vital to reinforce what has been said and to introduce new words and ideas.

■ How does your carer respond to your child? Are they genuinely interested in what your child has to say? Do they encourage your child to speak and allow them to initiate conversations?

Intellectual skills

Intellectual development involves the process of gaining, storing and retrieving information. Intellectual development allows the child to think for themselves, to concentrate and to solve problems. Does your child's carer:

■ provide opportunities and resources which encourage them to be curious? Is the environment in which they work welcoming, colourful and interesting? Does the carer provide posters, pictures, games and books which encourage your child to observe and explore?

■ interact with the children, encouraging them to see how things work or fit together? Do they ask questions which are thought provoking and demonstrate how to use certain pieces of equipment?

■ understand the importance of repetition and how to develop activities so that they become more and more challenging without pushing too much or risk being over complex?

■ know how to encourage your child to explore their senses and to use these senses on a daily basis in order to explore the world around them?

Literacy skills

Literacy involves the child's ability to read and write. Young children will need effective language and communication skills (see previous list) before they are in a position to develop literacy skills. In order for a child to develop their literacy skills you will need to satisfy yourself that your child's carer:

■ talks to and listens to your child. Verbal communication is vital for young children to form words and learn sounds;

■ shares books with your child. Children need to see adults reading in order for them to gain a positive attitude towards books. It is important that your child's carer has a love of books and that they share this love with the children. Ask to look at the kind of books on offer. Are they varied and do they appeal to a wide age range? Are there factual books as well as story books. Will your child have access to poems and rhymes?

■ understands your views on television. Is your child allowed to watch television? Although some parents are opposed to their children watching television and, admittedly the amount of viewing they have access to should be limited; in moderation it can be an invaluable learning source for literacy skills. Make sure that your carer chooses the programmes carefully but, by watching appropriate children's programmes together, useful skills can be encouraged.

Numeracy skills

Numeracy skills involve the confidence and competence to deal with numbers including problem solving, counting and measuring. Young children can be taught how to count through daily repetition such as when singing songs or reciting numbers while climbing steps. Your child's numeracy skills can be enhanced and improved in the following ways:

- If their carer provides activities that promote and encourage the understanding of numbers. These include games such as snakes and ladders, dominoes, snap and lotto.

- Simple activities, such as pairing socks, gloves and mittens or role play and dressing up all encourage children to sort and match up similar objects.

- Find out whether your child will have the opportunity to measure and weigh, this can be done when taking part in baking sessions or when shopping.

- Nurseries often have sand pits and water trays and these can be invaluable for encouraging children to learn about volume and capacity. Allowing children to fill and empty containers of various sizes will encourage them to learn about measurements.

REAL-LIFE EXPERIENCES

Nothing takes the place of real-life experiences. All the toys and play equipment in the world, though useful and exciting, should never be allowed to take the place of real-life experiences and whenever possible children should be allowed the freedom to explore the world around them and to experience real-life opportunities.

All areas of a child's development including sensory, intellectual, physical, and communication are improved when a child has the chance to take part in these kinds of experiences.

TIP

Children learn by doing. Make sure that the carer you choose allows the children the opportunity for 'hands on' experiences. Enquire about the learning experiences, outings and activities your child will have access to.

6

Daily Routines

UNDERSTANDING ROUTINES

Children need routines to help them feel settled and secure. Your child's routine will depend largely on the kind of daycare you choose for them. If you opt for childcare in your own home, for example if you employ the services of a nanny, then you will be able to set your own routine giving your own preferences and choices. However if you decide to take your child to a childminder or nursery setting then they will have to fit into an already established routine and you may find yourself having to make some compromises. For example, if you employ a nanny your child will be able to continue having their breakfast at 9am if this is what they are used to. However, if you take your child to a childminder they may have to have their breakfast slightly earlier or later if the childminder has to take children to school for 9am.

Familiarising yourself with the routine

Regardless of the kind of carer you choose it is important that you familiarise yourself with the setting's routines and make sure that, although the routine may need to be structured, it is also flexible. For example, how do you feel about set sleeping patterns for all children regardless of whether they need a sleep or not? Some nurseries put young children to sleep at certain times of the day, every day, regardless of whether the child needs a nap or not. They may also wake a child for feeding rather than allow them to sleep and feed them when they wake up. It is important that you are aware of these types of routines and if you are not happy with them then choose a different carer. Carers *should* always cater for each child's individual needs and a good carer would not force a child to take a nap or a tired child to eat.

Routines should be planned appropriately for the age and stage of development of the children being cared for with time throughout the day for free play, where the child is allowed to choose what they would like to do, and structured play when the child is encouraged to take part in supervised activities such as arts and crafts.

PARENTAL PREFERENCES

Whenever possible, your preferences as a parent should be taken into account. Whatever type of childcare you choose you have the right to expect your views to be respected and your wishes followed. There may of course be times when compromises will have to be made and you must bear in mind that childcare practitioners have an obligation to a number of families and not just yours!

There will be many areas of your child's daily care into which you want to have an input. You have every right to voice your opinions and request that certain things are done how you prefer. However, you would be well advised to steer clear of laying down too many rules and regulations for your chosen childcare practitioner to follow. If you have chosen well you should already be relatively sure that the person or persons you are trusting with the care of your child will be well suited to do so, therefore it will be unnecessary for you to go through every single detail of your child's daily routine and insist on things being done 'your way'. If every parent insisted on things being done 'their way' then the practitioner's job would be impossible!

Family input

Children first begin to learn from their parents in the home setting. In order for children to develop into healthy, happy and well-adjusted adults it is important that the adults around them, both parents and carers, provide them with a loving environment and that they set good examples at all times. It is a sad fact of life that this is not always the case. Children can be exposed to poor quality care both in the home setting and in daycare. There are three main ways of caring for children. These are:

1. A lax, lenient approach where children are allowed to do more or less as they please. Parents and carers have little control over the child and there are few, if any, rules or boundaries.

2. A consistent, loving environment where the children are listened to, welcomed and valued.

3. A strict, overpowering environment with many rules and restrictions and little encouragement, praise or recognition.

Children who are cared for in either a lax or strict environment, although having very different types of carers, will experience similar feelings such as:

■ rebellion;
■ anger;
■ nervousness;
■ indecision.

These are not positive feelings which children should be experiencing and it is important that parents work together with the carers to ensure that the children are happy and confident and that the care they receive has the following positive effects on them:

■ confidence;
■ independence;
■ responsibility;
■ self-control;
■ cooperation;
■ awareness.

CHILD PREFERENCES

If given the choice, it is probably true to say that most children would opt for their carer to be lenient, issuing few, if any rules and allowing them a free run to do as they like! In theory this may sound good to a child. However, in principle, the effects of this type of parenting can be profound and devastating. All children need rules and boundaries in order for them to feel safe and secure. Parents are responsible for the care and well being of the children and, as such, are in a position to choose wisely how they feel their children should be brought up. Although there is nothing wrong with allowing a child choices and preferences, it is important to remember that giving in to them all the time will result in the child:

- becoming insecure;
- having low self-esteem;
- becoming worried at making mistakes or making the wrong choices;
- showing aggression;
- lacking in self-control;
- becoming domineering and demanding;
- showing little understanding of right and wrong.

So, what happens when your child starts making demands on you or their carer? Will you be the kind of parent who thinks that your child should be able to make their opinions and preferences known and that it is acceptable for them to get their own way or do you think this is rude and should be discouraged?

Rest assured children *do* have preferences and if they think they can get away with it then they will make unreasonable demands on those around them. After all, we all like having our own way don't we? Children are no exception.

The problems of course appear when you, the parent, say one thing and your child's carer says another. Who should the child listen to? 'Me, of course' I hear you say. But what if pleasing you makes your child happy, but is difficult for the practitioner to cope with? Children are very adept at 'playing adults off against one another' and this should be avoided at all costs.

To ensure that your child does not use the age-old tactic of getting their own way by saying, for example, to you that their 'carer allows them to watch television while eating their tea' and tells their carer that 'mummy always lets them have sweets before lunch', then you should talk to your child's carer about any issues like this which may arise. If you and the carer have an understanding of what each other will and will not allow then you can avoid this problem all together.

Expressing wishes and making choices

How or if a child makes their preferences known will depend on the nature of the child. A shy child, for example, may find the whole concept of daycare overwhelming and expressing their wishes will be the very last thing on their mind. A competent carer will recognise this and encourage the child to make choices and gradually bring them out of their shell.

A spirited child with lots of confidence will have no trouble being heard and will probably let their carer know very early on exactly what they prefer and an easy-going child tends to thrive in any kind of childcare setting and will be happy to go along with whatever is on offer. Whatever kind of child you have their carer should be confident in ensuring that they are treated as an individual, shown equal concern and given equal opportunities.

FOOD AND DRINK

Most parents will ask for a healthy, balanced diet for their children. This leads me to think that they expect the average childcare practitioner to feed the children on burgers and chips every day. Childminders, nannies and nursery staff will all be proficient at providing and preparing fresh, nutritional foods and they will endeavour to feed the children on a healthy, balanced diet. This does not mean however that there won't be some treats included along the way.

Of course, parents have the right to request that their children have no sweets or fizzy drinks (most childcare practitioners would not offer these anyway on a regular basis) although it is perhaps stretching things a little too far by insisting that they do not have any puddings, preferring the child to have only fruit. Problems occur here when the child witnesses others having apple pie and custard or rice pudding and get angry and frustrated when they are presented with a piece of fruit.

Parental preferences, though perfectly acceptable, should not result in making a child appear 'different' from the others in the care and, of course, your own preferences of no puddings, only fruit, cannot be imposed on the other children attending the setting. Providing the children have a reasonable amount of fruit throughout the day, is a pudding really going to have a detrimental affect on your child's overall well being?

Food at home and in the daycare setting

It is not my place to instruct parents on what to feed their children and, if you feel very strongly about certain issues with regard to food and drink, then you should let your child's carer know. However you should be prepared for the battle you may get from your child if they are old enough to understand that they are not being offered the same as everyone else in the setting! This is a problem that you will have to sort out and you should never expect other parents or children to conform to your requests just to appease your child.

In my experience, parents often insist on fresh fruit and vegetables for their child, when they know that it will be a battle of wills for the carer to get them to eat. This is simply because they themselves do not cook healthy food at home, relying on pre-packed meals and sandwiches. Insisting that their child gets everything they need for a healthy diet while at the child-minder's or nursery gives them the excuse to opt out of healthy living at home. After all their child will have had their daily intake of fruit and vegetables so where is the harm in giving them a piece of chocolate cake for supper?

It is only fair, if you are intending to insist that your child's carer only offers healthy food, that you do the same at home. This will ensure that your child is getting a healthy, balanced diet all of the time and will encourage them to eat well. It will also ensure that they do not see daycare as providers of awful food and home as offering good food!

Questions about mealtimes

There are certain things that you should be looking for with regard to mealtimes and it is a good idea to ask questions such as:

- What kind of meals are provided? Are they varied and nutritious?

- Does the carer take into account child preferences?

- Can the carer cater for special diets such as vegetarian?

- Can the carer cater for children with allergies such as a milk intolerance?

- Are mealtimes pleasant, sociable and unhurried?

■ Are the children suitably supervised during mealtimes?

■ Are table manners actively encouraged?

■ Will the carer support your decision to continue breastfeeding your baby and, if so, what arrangements will be made?

■ How are babies fed in the setting? Carers should hold babies when bottle feeding and never prop a child up with a bottle or deprive them of human contact.

■ If your child is a fussy eater are you welcome to provide your own food and, if so what arrangements are made to enable you to do this?

■ Will you need to supply your baby with formula milk and weaning foods?

■ Does the setting have adequate, safe equipment for mealtimes such as highchairs with harnesses, feeding cups and children's cutlery?

SLEEP AND REST

This is a difficult one and one where both sides of the argument are plain to see. In my opinion, the matter of sleep and rest times should be decided by the child. A child will only sleep if they are tired. I have tried unsuccessfully for years to get parents to understand that, although I cannot force a tired child to stay awake, nor can I make a wide-awake child go to sleep. There are two very different types of parents when it comes to allowing children adequate sleep and rest patterns. Simply put, there are those parents who don't want their children to sleep during the day, and those who do.

No sleep

Parents who refuse to allow their child to sleep during the day have their own agenda. Usually it is because they want them to go straight to bed when they get home. Ask yourself do you fall into this trap? Are you the kind of parent who, after a tiring day at work, needs to put their feet up with a glass of wine with no child distractions? This is not a criticism; it is a question. What you must realise, however, is that by insisting that your child spends a full day, perhaps from 7.30am to 6pm in childcare where they are constantly playing and taking part in activities, you are effectively wearing them out by insisting that they do not sleep during the day. It is a little unfair of you to expect your child's carer to keep your exhausted child awake all day just so that you can put them straight to bed when you get home.

There is no such thing as an average child, therefore it is probably true to say that there is no such thing as an average child's daily sleep pattern. Some two-year-olds will sleep for two hours in an afternoon and have no trouble going to bed at 7pm, while others who have no sleep during the day will still be active at 10pm.

I have had parents say to me, 'Do not let my child sleep during the day – they won't go to bed at night.' If I point out that their child is so tired that they fall asleep sat up while taking part in an activity or they are too tired to eat the parent will reply 'Allow them five minutes and not a minute more!' This is, of course, not the answer and my suggestion to parents who have children who refuse to go to bed at night is to work with, not against, their child's carer. Talk things through honestly. It may be that when you are at home with your child yourself you do allow them to sleep; this makes patterns difficult to establish and allowing a child an afternoon nap three days per week when you are with them but insisting that the carer refuses them sleep on the other four days is both confusing and upsetting for the child.

Must sleep

This is just as difficult to maintain as keeping a tired child awake and, once again, it will probably be down to your preference as a parent rather than that of your child. Parents who want their children to sleep during the day will again do so for a number of reasons.

- The don't want a tired, crying child at teatime.
- They think it is better for the child.
- They want to keep the child up so that they can play with them when they get home.

Children may sleep at home during the day when they are in their own familiar surroundings. However the noise factor alone in some nurseries and childminding settings may put some children off having an afternoon nap. This is something you should bear in mind and talk through with your chosen practitioner.

Work out a suitable plan that you and your child's childminder, nanny or nursery nurse can implement with you and be prepared to change this plan as and when necessary to suit the growing needs of your child.

SETTLING YOUR CHILD INTO THE SETTING

When you have made the all-important decision of finding the right childcare for your needs the next thing you will inevitably need to know is how to make your chosen childcare work for you and your child. Leaving your child with a carer is a big step for both of you and you will need to give yourself and your child time to adjust to the new arrangements. There are several ways that will help you and your child to make the transition into the new routine:

- Try to visit your chosen childcare facility a few times before the placement begins. Build up the amount of time that your child spends with their new carer over a period of time. At the first visit perhaps you could sit in the background watching while they find their feet for about half and hour or so. On the next visit try leaving the setting completely for half an hour then on the third and subsequent visits build on this time extending it to an hour, then a morning and finally a full day.

- When choosing the day you will return to work, think about your child's routine. If possible, arrange for your first day to be a Wednesday so that your child only has a 'short' week initially building up to a full week the next.

- Talk to your child. Obviously this will depend on their age and stage of understanding but many toddlers and school-age children will cope better if you explain any changes to them.

- Help your child to help themselves. Being independent will boost a child's confidence immeasurably and, if they can tie their own shoe laces, wipe their own nose and go to the toilet independently this may go a long way to helping them to settle in quickly. Children who are shy and lack confidence may be reluctant to ask for help and by preparing them in advance and teaching them simple self-help tasks you will eliminate this problem.

■ Give yourself plenty of time when dropping your child off. It is not a good idea to hang around indefinitely as long drawn out goodbyes are not good for anyone. However, giving yourself an extra five minutes to encourage your child to show you the things they enjoy doing will help to make the transition easier. Rushing in, dumping your child and rushing back out again should be avoided at all costs.

■ Allow the carer to help as much as possible. Sitting in a corner with your hysterical child clinging to your neck is not the answer. The carer will probably have had lots of experience at settling children into the setting and they will be very aware of the different strategies which may work.

■ Allow your child to take a comfort object with them if this helps. A teddy bear, favourite toy or blanket may be the security your child needs initially and you should be prepared to allow them to take something they recognise from home if this helps them to settle.

■ Resist the urge to look sad yourself. Children are very adept at picking up on moods and they will sense your apprehension and respond to this. Try to be as upbeat as possible and reassure your child that they will have a good time.

■ Stay positive.

The goodbye routine

Try to allow yourself plenty of time when dropping your child off with their carer. Although it is not a good idea to prolong leaving as this can often upset a child more, neither should you sneak off while your child isn't looking or if they are engrossed in an activity as this may lead to distrust and feelings of abandonment.

Try to stick to a set 'goodbye' routine each morning to enable your child to be aware of what is happening.

- Allow yourself plenty of time.

- Speak to the staff or carer in an upbeat, happy tone. Even if you are feeling miserable at having to leave your child, don't let this be apparent to them as children often pick up on the way the adults are feeling and this will give off negative vibes.

- Encourage your child to show you what they have been doing.

- Engage your child in their favourite activity.

- Tell your child you are leaving, kiss them and say 'goodbye'.

- Leave when you say you are going to. If your child cries, let the carer deal with them but still leave. By staying longer you are effectively rewarding your child's tears and this will make the problem worse.

- Explain where you are going. If your child is old enough to understand then explain to them that you are going to work so that they know why you are leaving them and when you will be back.

■ Reassure yourself that your child is fine by telephoning the setting. Parents find this particularly helpful if they have left their child crying. It is important to remember that most children stop crying a few minutes after their parents have left and by telephoning the setting you will be reassured that your child is happy thereby eliminating the need for you to worry about them all day.

It is important to take comfort from the fact that your child does not cry when you leave them in the childcare setting. This may seem like obvious advice but I am constantly surprised at how many parents are only happy when their child 'cries after them' when they drop them off. I have even had parents return to the setting several times just to say 'goodbye' in an attempt to get them to cry.

It is surely much better for the parent to leave a happy, contented child, safe in the knowledge that they are having a good time, than allowing feelings of guilt to get in the way, triggering a selfish need to have the child 'pine after' them. Making your child cry adds to the carers' already busy job because they then have to spend time calming down the upset child when they really ought to be serving breakfast.

SAFETY ISSUES

Safety with regard to environment and equipment is something that you will have satisfied yourself with prior to registering your child in your preferred setting. You will need to be sure that the provider you have chosen has a proven track record for ensuring the safety of the children in their care and it is the job of Ofsted to register and inspect all childminders and nurseries to ensure that all safety regulations are adhered to.

In addition to the safety of the toys and equipment provided you will also need to be sure that the person you are trusting with the care of your child is suitable to be in contact with young children and, once again, this is where Ofsted's checks will provide you with the necessary reassurance. Some of the checks that Ofsted carry out on providers include:

- Criminal Records Bureau (CRB) check;

- checks with the social services department where the registered person has lived for the last five years;

- references;

- medical report from the registered persons GP (for child-minders and managers of daycare nurseries).

Once again it pays to choose a *registered* childcare provider in order to be absolutely certain that the person has satisfied the rigorous checks necessary before registration is granted.

SPECIAL EDUCATIONAL NEEDS AND DISABILITIES

It is a necessary requirement for all childcare providers to meet the requirements of the Disability Discrimination Act 1995. Reasonable adjustments must be made to include disabled children in the setting and no child should be treated less favourably than someone else due to their disability. Before expecting a childcare provider to understand the meaning of 'equal opportunity', however, it is important that parents understand it. Treating children 'equally' does *not* mean treating them all the same.

Any parent choosing childcare will be faced with a difficult task. If you are the parent of a disabled child or one who has special educational needs then this task will be made all the more difficult. How can you be sure that the carer you find will provide your child with the necessary additional care they may require? Your child may require more support from the carer than the other children and you will inevitably feel anxious and concerned that this may not happen.

The easiest way around this potential problem is to discuss your worries and concerns with your chosen practitioner and work out a suitable strategy together. You should endeavour to share as much information with your child's carer, about their disability, as possible. Knowledge is after all very powerful and the more information the practitioner has about your child's needs the better equipped they will be to care for them.

There are many childminders, nannies and nursery nurses who are specially trained in caring for disabled children or those with special educational needs and, depending on the severity, you may like to source a practitioner who has the skills and experience your child requires.

Questions to ask

When looking for childcare for a child with special educational needs or a disability you may like to consider the following points:

- Does the childcare facility have full access for children with physical disabilities such as no steps and wide doors for wheelchair users?

- Has the provider any experience in caring for children with special needs or a disability?

- Do the toys and equipment available provide sufficient stimulation for your child?

- Can the carer access specially adapted toys and equipment if these are necessary?

- How does the carer feel about looking after older children who are not toilet trained?

- Is the carer enthusiastic about caring for a child with special needs or a disability and willing to take any extra necessary training to help them carry out their duties to the best of their ability?

- Is the carer willing to work with you to provide the best possible care for your child?

- Is the carer comfortable dealing with the challenges that some types of disabilities or medical conditions may pose?

- Is the carer willing to liaise with trained professionals when necessary?

HOLIDAYS

Everyone needs a break at some point in their working lives to switch off, rest and recharge their batteries. You may be one of those people who count the weeks, days and hours to your next holiday in order to get through the stress and turmoil of your everyday working life. On the other hand, you may thrive on the cut and thrust of the boardroom. You may be a workaholic who sees no reason why anyone should need to go on holiday. As a parent I personally believe that everyone with a family should allow themselves time to spend with their children.

Holidays needn't be expensive monthly jaunts to the Caribbean. A few days in a tent in wet Wales may work just as well, providing you allow yourself to enjoy time away from work to relax and take time out with your children.

Holidays, though essential, do however cause headaches when it comes to childcare arrangements.

Parent's holiday

There are several ways that you can ensure that your holiday does not upset the arrangements you have with your child's carer.

■ Give your carer ample notice. Many contracts will state the required notice period but, if you are planning a holiday months in advance, let your child's carer know so that they can plan their own holidays around you if possible.

■ Be prepared to pay for your child's place when you go on holiday. Many childminders, nannies and nurseries insist on being paid if you take your child out of care to go on holiday.

■ Be organised. Ask your child's carer if they have any holidays planned and, whenever possible, try to plan them together so that disruption to your and your child's usual routine can be kept to a minimum.

Carer's holiday

Even if you are one of those parents who thrive on work and see no reason for a holiday, *never* assume that your childminder or nanny should feel the same way. Rest assured they will not be willing to work 52 weeks of the year just because you love work so much! Try to avoid criticism, recognise that they have earned their holiday and allow them to enjoy their break in peace without feeling guilty or awkward because you feel they have let you down.

A professional practitioner will plan their holidays well in advance and give you lots of notice. If you can't plan your own holidays at the same time then this will allow you ample opportunity to make alternative arrangements to cover the holiday period. Choosing to leave your child in a nursery setting will eliminate the potential problems caused by holiday leave as staff are usually on hand to cover holidays.

Holiday charges

The vast majority of childminders take very few holidays. In my experience they tend to stick to a maximum of four or five weeks, many of which will probably include Bank Holidays such as Christmas. Home-based child carers will either charge you:

- in full when they go on holiday;
- half when they go on holiday;
- nothing when they go on holiday.

It will be up to you to negotiate with the practitioner what, if any, fees will be payable when they are unavailable to work due to holidays. Childminders are self-employed and are therefore not actually entitled to holiday pay, however, many feel that they have the right to charge something for their holidays in line with their employed customers. How you deal with this request is entirely up to you and you should discuss this before any placement begins.

Childminders who do not charge for holidays may be reluctant to take time off as holidays may be a luxury they can ill afford if it means they have no wages coming in for a couple of weeks. This is however not an ideal situation and, if your chosen practitioner requests some holiday pay, think carefully before refusing their request. Do you get paid when you are on holiday? Ideally parents and practitioners will come to some arrangement whereby some, if not all, of the holidays taken are paid for.

POTTY TRAINING

When should a child be out of nappies? If I had a £1 coin for every time I have been asked this question I would be a very rich woman indeed. Potty training a child is not easy. It requires planning, dedication and perseverance from *everyone* responsible for caring for the child.

Potty training should be seen as a team effort whereby all the main players i.e. the child, the parents and the carers, work together. As a parent there is little point in you leaving this task to your child's practitioner; it is essential that you work with your child's carer to devise a suitable plan to introduce the potty and make the transition from nappies to toilet a successful one.

If you are the kind of parent who thinks that it is better to take the lead from your child when it comes to potty training, and prefer to wait until they show an interest and understanding of leaving nappies behind then you will be heading for trouble if you enrol your child in a nursery whose policy is to start potty training a child as soon as they hit their second birthday!

Likewise you will have similar problems if you think your child is ready to start using the potty but the carer insists on keeping your child in nappies.

You may like to consider asking some of the questions below with regard to potty training.

- Who is responsible for providing nappies? If the answer to this is the carer you can be assured that they will be more keen to potty train your child than if they insist that you provide the nappies. It is in the carer's interests to get your child potty trained quickly if only from the point of view of expenditure.

- Ask the carer if they have a policy with regard to potty training. For example, do they begin to potty train children depending on their age or do they prefer to take into account the child's progress and understanding?

- What are the strategies for toilet training?

- Does the carer provide potties, child seats for toilets and steps to enable children to reach an adult toilet safely? Are you expected to provide any of this equipment?

- How does the carer encourage success when it comes to potty training? Are any rewards offered?

- What 'language' is used in the setting with regard to bodily functions? Silly as this sounds children can be easily confused if the terms used at home are different from those used in the childcare setting and it is important to be consistent.

When is a child ready to leave nappies behind?

The simple answer to this is when *they* are ready! I have met countless numbers of parents who have worried that their two-year-old shows no interest in sitting on a potty whatsoever. My answer to this is:

- give them time;
- introduce the child to the potty slowly;
- do not force the issue;
- persevere.

I have noticed a trend in children becoming 'dry' later and later. When my own children were young they were allowed to start playgroup at two-and-a-half years old *providing* they were out of nappies. Nowadays however children can start playgroup at two-and-a-half years old *regardless* of whether they are out of nappies or not and surprisingly many of the children still wear a nappy after this age.

Many theories have been offered to try to explain the reasoning behind this.

- More and more mothers are working now and don't have the time to potty train their children.

- Children are lazier.

- It is more socially acceptable for a child to still be wearing a nappy at three years old than it was in the past.

■ It is more difficult to train a child who wears disposable nappies as they do not feel wet and uncomfortable as they used to in traditional 'terry' nappies.

Whatever the reason behind the trend in children wearing nappies longer is not really the issue. What is important is that parents and practitioners work *together* in order to help the child to understand the importance of a toilet training routine. There is little benefit in potty training a child while they are in the childminding setting and then, immediately they get home, they are put straight back into a nappy. Mixed messages are given to the child in abundance in this kind of scenario! It is important that you are honest and open with your child's carer in order to provide a potty training routine that your child can understand and that both you and the carer can implement.

Potty training has always been a bone of contention for child carers. Some parents expect the carer to potty train their child and, if this is proving difficult or the carer requests some form of training pants/nappy in the interim, parents may become annoyed. The reasons for this are varied.

■ They feel their child will take longer to train.
■ They see training pants as another form of nappy thereby defeating the object of getting the child 'dry'.
■ They do not like the expense involved in buying training pants.
■ They feel the job of potty training is down to the carer.

What I would say to the parents who feel like this is put yourself in your carer's position.

- They may be caring for several children who are all potty training at the same time making the job more difficult.

- They will have a busy schedule to stick to with school runs, playgroup, trips etc., all of which make potty training more difficult.

- From a health and hygiene point of view they cannot have dozens of wet patches throughout their premises where your child, and perhaps others, have had 'accidents'.

TIP

The important thing to remember here is to talk to your child's carer and work **with** *rather than* **against** *them. Try to make their job as easy as possible and the success rate for potty training will be much higher.*

WHOSE SETTING IS IT?

As a parent paying for childcare you may sometimes feel that you have the upper hand and may, at times, be guilty of making demands. In my experience this seems to happen more often in a childminding setting rather than in a nursery as there is only one practitioner to 'deal with'.

It is important for you to remember that your childminder offers a service. You are not obliged to take up their offer and, if you feel they are not carrying out your wishes, you do have the option to find alternative arrangements. This is not to say that you should storm out every time a disagreement comes to light and, whenever possible, you would be advised to talk to your childminder and find a suitable solution to any problems.

There is more about dealing with issues and concerns in Chapter 10. However, what is very important is that you remember first and foremost that you do not *employ* a childminder. They are self-employed and, as I have said before, they offer a service. You need to be sure that the service they offer is the right one for you prior to signing contracts but, after the placement begins, you should not expect your child's carer to give into your additional requests or take kindly to your suggestions if they clearly cannot be met.

7

Illness

WHEN THE CHILD IS ILL

As a mother myself the thought of leaving my own children when they are ill is something which I personally would never contemplate. However, I do understand that in some circumstances parents have difficulty getting time off work. It may be that you do not have a very understanding boss or meetings or appointments with important clients may have been made. Any one of these reasons may play heavily on your mind and you may end up convincing yourself that your child will be alright without you and that you are needed more at work. But where exactly does this leave your child's practitioner? An already demanding job of caring for children who are not ill is made considerably more difficult if parents expect them to care for a child who is, at best, under the weather and, at worst, too poorly to mix with others.

Childminders often have several children to care for of varying ages but unfortunately this is not something some parents seem to take into account. Nurseries may have anything up to and sometimes over 30 children to care for and will not be best pleased if you leave a sick child with them.

Employing a nanny is perhaps the only way you can be sure that your child will have someone available to care for them should they be ill but even this comes with its own problems as the nanny may well catch the illness themselves and need time off work, adding to your childcare problems.

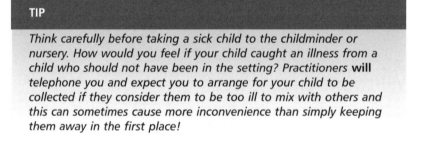

TIP

*Think carefully before taking a sick child to the childminder or nursery. How would you feel if your child caught an illness from a child who should not have been in the setting? Practitioners **will** telephone you and expect you to arrange for your child to be collected if they consider them to be too ill to mix with others and this can sometimes cause more inconvenience than simply keeping them away in the first place!*

Often by keeping your child at home with you for a short period of time, perhaps only 24 hours, this can make all the difference between the child feeling under the weather and them developing something more serious because they have been denied adequate time to rest and bounce back to complete health.

Bringing a sick child into a childminder's home or nursery setting is not only bad for the child themselves, but also adds to the problems of infecting both the carers and the other children present.

Parents' attitudes

Parents differ tremendously in the way they handle the problems which arise when their child is ill. Unfortunately, some consider it bad enough having to take time off in their busy work schedule at all but to do so in order to nurse a sick child who is vomiting everywhere and can't stop crying is not an attractive proposition for some of today's parents.

Others will happily stay at home and nurse their children until they are fit and well again. The attitude to sick children is not so much down to the kind of job the parents have as to the kind of nurturing instinct they possess. I am not trying to say that a parent who stays at home with their ill child is a *better* parent than one who expects them to soldier on, just that their priorities are different. Parenting comes in all shapes and sizes and there is no right or wrong way of bringing up children. What works admirably for one family may be a complete waste of time for another. What is important however is that working parents take the time to consider *everyone* involved when they make their decision. You and your child will not be the only people affected by the decision you make. The practitioners and other children need to be considered, particularly in the case of sick children.

How sick is sick?

How sick does a child have to be to stay at home? This is truly the million dollar question. This question is asked by working parents the world over every day. By keeping your child at home every time they sneeze you risk complicating your working life unnecessarily, however, by insisting that your child attends daycare when they are obviously unwell, will make enemies of the staff not to mention other parents whose children are in attendance.

Questions to ask

To enable you to satisfactorily assess whether your child should be at home or not you may like to ask yourself the following questions and, more importantly, answer them *truthfully*.

- Is your child able to take part in the usual daily routine provided by the carer? If your child is under the weather, tired or listless and appears to want nothing more strenuous to do than lie on the sofa then it is unfair to him, your carer and the other children to insist that he attends daycare.

- Does your child have a contagious illness? If the answer to this question is yes then you *must* keep him at home (see list of contagious illnesses on page 123).

- Are you able to collect your child should their symptoms become worse as the day progresses? If you do decide to take a risk and send your child to their carer you must inform them of your suspicions and make yourself available should you be required to collect your child if their symptoms become worse.

- If you are in any doubt, telephone your child's carer and ask their advice. Professional carers are highly unlikely to tell you not to bring your child to the setting if they do not pose a risk to others.

Coughs and colds are an inevitable part of everyday life and children can have as many as six colds a year, sometimes more. A child is not usually expected to stay away from the daycare setting if they are suffering from a simple cold. However if the cold is teamed with a temperature, listlessness and lethargy then they should be kept at home.

Providing children are able to mix and play happily with others when they have a cold they should be welcome in the setting. However you should not expect your child's carer to take on the role of nurse and, if you are in any doubt about their suitability to mix with other children, give the practitioner a courtesy telephone call and ask for their advice. Being told your child is unwell at the outset is preferable to being called from your desk to collect them after you have just spent a long time in the rush hour traffic!

Keeping the child home

So, we have decided that the average cold is par for the course and rarely results in a child needing to be kept at home. So what kinds of illness should you be looking for which will make your child unwelcome in a childcare setting?

It is worth bearing in mind that, as a condition of registration, childcare practitioners are not allowed to care for children who have an infectious illness.

Illnesses which will result in your child being kept away from the setting are:

- vomiting;
- diarrhoea;
- chicken pox;
- measles;
- conjunctivitis;
- food poisoning;

- gastro-enteritis;
- meningitis;
- rubella;
- mumps;
- impetigo;
- head lice;
- threadworms;
- whooping cough.

This list is by no means exhaustive and you should, on the whole, use your common sense when deciding whether your child is well enough to be left in a childcare setting or not. Your childcare practitioner or local health authority should be able to furnish you with an up-to-date list of contagious illnesses which will result in your child being kept away from the setting.

If your child has been prescribed an antibiotic allow the medicine time to take effect for between 24 and 48 hours before re-introducing your child to the setting.

Children may sometimes contract infections which, although not contagious, it may still be better to keep the child at home at least until the medication they have been prescribed can take effect and ease any pain they may be experiencing, for example in the case of an ear infection.

Avoid the temptation to rush your child back to good health, this will invariably make things worse and by pressurising a child into recovering too quickly and sending them back into the childcare setting before they are properly recuperated, you risk re-infecting them and prolonging the illness.

❝ *Be practical when it comes to expecting too much from your child's carer when the child is ill. Practitioners generally have a lot of experience of sick children and will be able to tell at a glance whether the child is well enough to be in the setting, so trying to fool them is not your best option.*

In the past I have had a child brought to me looking pale and listless who has told me, the minute they have got through the door, that they have been 'sick all night'. The parent promptly brushed off the child's comment saying, 'No, you haven't, you just feel sick because you haven't had any breakfast yet and your tummy is empty'. Less then 30 minutes later, after serving breakfast, the child promptly vomited all over the floor. When I telephoned the parent to ask them to collect their child, I was told how 'inconvenient' it was because they had only just arrived at work.

This kind of cover up from the parent is completely unhelpful to the child, the carer and ultimately themselves. Parents should never expect carers to look after a sick child. Think how annoyed you would be if your child caught something from another child who should not have been in the setting due to a illness or contagious disease. ❞

WHAT KIND OF PARENT ARE YOU?

How would you react if your child's childminder or nursery nurse telephoned you at work to inform you that your child seems to have contracted chicken pox? Would you:

- tell them to deal with it?

- ask them what they expect you to do?

- become defensive and say that she must have contracted them from someone else in the setting?

- tell them that as she is already contagious they may as well keep her there?

- drop the telephone, run around like a headless chicken and arrive at the setting at breakneck speed to collect your spotty child?

- tell them you will be with them in half an hour?

How you answer this question says a lot about the kind of parent you are, the type of employer you have – this can have a huge impact on the way you respond to your child's illness – and what you expect from the sort of childcare you have chosen.

Ideally you will listen to what the practitioner is telling you and make arrangements to collect your child as soon as possible. Don't make excuses or requests that will be awkward for the practitioner to carry out and remember that they have an obligation to *all* the children in their care.

Listen to the practitioner when they tell you how long your child will need to be away from the setting to ensure that they are not contagious to other children, and make alternative arrangements for the care of your child during this time if you are unable to take the time off work. Children will inevitably get sick from time to time and this usually happens at the most inconvenient times. By having a back up plan you can eliminate any potential major headaches and ensure that your work and family life run smoothly.

One of the most important things to remember is that your child care practitioner is **NOT** responsible for caring for your sick child and you should never expect them to do so. Avoid confrontations and embarrassment by refraining from taking your child to the childminder or nursery setting if they are obviously unwell. Children may become ill during the day while already in daycare and, if this is the case, make yourself available to the practitioner and sort out arrangements for your child to be collected as soon as possible. Rest assured a professional practitioner will not bother you at work unless they are concerned about your child.

TIP

When your child is ill, you should ideally follow these tips.

■ *Make yourself available if your child's carer telephones you at work.*

■ *Listen to what the practitioner has to say and decide together the best course of action.*

■ *If the practitioner requests that you collect your child immediately due to vomiting or a highly contagious illness then make sure you heed this request.*

■ *Ask the practitioner how long they consider your child should be kept away from the setting.*

■ *Remember that your child's carer has an obligation to ensure the health of all the children in their care – not just yours.*

■ *Avoid being confrontational or making excuses. Children will become ill from time to time – accept this and deal with it.*

■ *Have a back up plan – make alternative childcare arrangements to implement in the case of illness in order for your work and family life to run as smoothly as possible.*

WHEN THE CARER IS ILL

It is inevitable, when they have come in contact with several sick children, that the practitioner themselves may succumb to illness. After all they are human. So, how do parents take the news that their child's carer is not well enough to look after their child? This will of course depend on the type of childcare you have opted for and whether or not you have arranged any back up cover for such events.

Obviously if you opt for childcare in a nursery provision then, as with holiday cover, staff illness should not pose a problem to you as the nursery should have sufficient cover for this kind of scenario. However, in extreme circumstances, perhaps in the event of an outbreak of vomiting and diarrhoea or food poisoning, it may be that several members of staff fall victim to the illness resulting in the nursery having to close for a few days. Once again in this kind of circumstance you will be left to find childcare cover yourself.

Some carers, such as nannies or childminders, may be able to help you with a back up plan by lining up someone who is willing to cover for them should they be unavailable. Childminders, for example, are often part of a close knit circle and, if vacancies are available, they may be able to arrange temporary cover for illness and holidays. Of course, you may feel quite strongly that you do not want your child's carer to have anything to do with sorting out back up cover for emergencies and, if this is the case, then you will have to deal with the situation yourself.

If you do allow your carer to sort out back up cover then you must be sure that the person providing the cover is suitable and that they are aware of your and your child's needs. *Never* leave the responsibility of checking out suitability of a back up carer to your usual practitioner.

As I have mentioned before, having a back up plan that you can put into action in such a situation is vital for your work and family life to run smoothly.

BACK UP PLANS

Try to refrain from being angry if your child's carer gets ill. Yes, it is inconvenient and yes, you will have to make alternative arrangements but we all succumb to illness at some point and it is probably true to say that the vast majority of childcare practitioners get ill through contracting something from the many children they are in contact with on a daily basis. Children's hygiene often leaves a lot to be desired and faced with runny noses, coughs and sneezes which are rarely stifled with a hand, and failure to wash hands thoroughly will result in illness and infection from time to time.

The simple fact of the matter is that you must be prepared for *when* your child's carer becomes ill not *if* they become ill. By thinking ahead and having a back up plan for the times when your child's carer is ill you will be able to put your plan swiftly into action, should the need arise, with as little disruption to your routine as possible.

Of course there are other reasons why your child's carer may need to take time off work other than through illness and these include the following.

- **Health problems**. In addition to illness none of us are immune to the odd appendicitis attack, which may result in surgery, or a broken limb which may result in us needing to take a few weeks off work, your child's carer included, and you must be prepared for all eventualities.

- **Jury duty**. Anyone who is called to do jury service has a legal obligation to do so. Often jury trials are short and simple but there is a possibility that some may last months or even years.

- **Emergencies**. Family or household emergencies can happen to anyone. If your childminder's mother is taken seriously ill or her home is struck by lightning, it is highly likely that she will require time off to deal with the situation.

- **Maternity leave**. You are not the only person allowed to be a mother and you may find yourself having to deal with your carer's own pregnancy issues. The carer may be more than happy to resume her duties once she has given birth but she will of course require some time off both before and after the baby is due.

Reliability

Reliability is more likely to come in the form of a nursery. Nurseries will have back up staff to provide cover for those who are taken ill or who are on holiday and the occasions where you are let down by a nursery are very rare. There is, of course, always the slight chance that they may have to close their doors in cases such as an outbreak of a serious health problem such as food poisoning, a financial crisis or serious issues with regard to the way the nursery setting is being run, which may result in registration being cancelled. However these situations are very rare and, on the whole, if you have no means whatsoever of sorting out any back up cover and you are unable to take time off work yourself if your child or carer is ill, then a nursery setting is probably the best option for you.

Putting back up cover in place

Now that you are aware of the reasons why back up cover is essential in order to cover the times when your regular carer is unavailable to look after your child, you will need to look at how to set up cover and use it successfully.

The way you set up cover will depend largely on the kind of job you have and your own network of available friends and family. If you are able to work from home then this is a good option for a couple of days if your child or their carer is ill. However, this may be impractical if your carer is on holiday for a couple of weeks. It is very difficult to come up with a single solution which will cover all eventualities throughout the day and therefore it is often a good idea to have a couple of plans to draw on. For example, you may be able to arrange to work from home for some of the days, take holiday for some and get your mother or a friend to help out for the rest.

Short-term back up plans

If your child's regular provider telephones you early in the morning to say that they have been vomiting all night and are unable to care for your child then you will need to think quickly and put your back up plan into action if you are to avoid major disruptions in your working life. By thinking in advance and planning ahead this should not be too much of a problem as you will already have sourced alternative childcare for this kind of situation. Your back up cover may consist of the following.

- Make arrangements with your employer to take advantage of any flexible working arrangements your company can offer. For example, you and your husband/partner may be able to juggle your hours so that one of you is able to stay at home to care for your child. This may take the form of working from home, reducing the number of hours you work or staggering the time you start and finish.

■ Enquire whether there are any emergency childcare facilities within your place of work. Many large companies offer childcare facilities for staff members and, even if you do not take advantage of this arrangement regularly, you may be able to utilise an available space for your child if your usual carer is unavailable.

■ Ask whether a family member or friend is able to care for your child. Often grandparents who are reluctant to take on the responsibility of childcare on a regular basis will be happy to step into the breach for a day or two to help out in an emergency.

■ See if you can take time off as holiday entitlement to carry you through the emergency period.

■ Ask your regular child carer if they know anyone who is willing to help out in the case of emergencies.

Long-term back up plans

It is usually relatively easy for parents to sort out short-term back up plans for the odd day when their usual carer is ill, however the real problems start if the carer needs to take a lot of time off, for example due to a medical problem or family situation. At times like these it needs to be said that you may find yourself having to reconsider your childcare arrangements. Despite the fact that your carer may be fantastic and you and your child may have grown very fond of her, if she is unable to provide the service you need you may have to look for alternative childcare. It is of course entirely up to you whether you look for temporary or permanent alternative childcare. If you chose temporary care bear in mind that your child may easily become attached to this new carer and feel the strain of leaving twice over.

8

Behaviour

THE IMPORTANCE OF A UNITED FRONT

Behaviour is one of the most important issues that parents and
carers will need to address and it is absolutely essential that you
and your child's carer are in complete agreement with regard to
issues surrounding behaviour. Children will test boundaries
and never more so than in the childcare setting when they are
'playing off' their parents and their carers. Children are often
confused as to who is actually in charge in the nursery or
childminding setting, particularly when their parents are
present at the beginning and end of each day.

Testing boundaries

Children are likely to resort to the kind of behaviour which they
are fully aware is unacceptable simply to get a reaction and see

who, if anyone, reprimands them. The easiest and most successful way of dealing with this kind of behaviour is to make sure you are aware of the settings policies, that you agree with them and that you ensure you assist the carer in utilising them. For example, if your child is openly misbehaving, or if their carer has asked them not to do something and they insist on carrying on, offer support and back up the carer, not your child! By allowing your child to get away with something which is clearly not acceptable, you risk undermining the authority of the carer, giving mixed messages to your child and causing confusion not just to your own child but to any others who may be present.

BEHAVIOUR POLICIES

It is essential that your child's carer has a behaviour policy for their setting which clearly states the kind of behaviour they will and will not tolerate and what, if any, sanctions are posed should the child continually show unacceptable behaviour. Always ask to see the setting's policy, read it and discuss it with your carer, making sure that you understand the content and agree with the conditions outlined. Many carers will ask you to sign to say you have read and understood their policy and, most importantly, that you will help to implement it. A behaviour policy is necessary for all the children in the setting to feel welcome and secure and it should take into account the ages of the children present and their level of understanding.

Behaviour signs

Your child and their carer or carers need to have a good relationship in order for them to get along and enjoy their time together. However it is a fact that no one is perfect and children rarely act like angels all of the time (even the shy ones who you thought would never step a foot wrong!) and there may be times when your child's behaviour needs to be put in check. When visiting childcare settings there are certain things you should be aware of in order to reassure yourself that the discipline procedures are effective.

The children should be:

- well behaved and doing as they are asked;
- responsive to the staff around them;
- happy to approach the staff, ask for help and make enquiries;
- happy in their play and learning;
- attentive;
- happy to play well in groups;
- respectful of their peers.

There may be cause for concern if the children present:

- ignore the requests of staff and disregard their instructions;
- are loud, boisterous and disruptive or quiet and withdrawn;
- are rude and badly behaved;
- are unhappy;
- are uninterested in the play and learning;
- fight and argue;
- show signs of bullying towards individuals;
- are unable to play well together.

PUNISHMENTS

Just as you must agree with the settings behaviour policy, so too must you be aware of, and agree, any punishments your child's carer may feel it necessary to impose. There is absolutely no point in agreeing to a behaviour policy if, at the very sign of your child being reprimanded, you come down on the carer like a tonne of bricks!

Unacceptable punishment

Childcare practitioners must NEVER smack a child in their care for any reason whatsoever. Nor must they use any other form of physical punishment such as:

- shaking;
- pushing;
- rough handling.

As a parent you should always be involved in the discipline of your child and there is no exception when your child is in daycare. You and your child's carer should discuss any negative behaviour issues and work out *together* how to deal with the situation.

It is important for you to think about the way you discipline your child at home and discuss these methods with your child's carer. However, you must bear in mind that the carer may have a number of other children to care for and her methods of managing behaviour must be clear and consistent in order for all the children to understand.

SANCTIONS FOR DEALING WITH INAPPROPRIATE BEHAVIOUR

Consider the following types of sanctions which are often used in a childcare setting to deal with unacceptable behaviour and see how you feel about them.

Using eye contact and facial expressions

Sometimes a child who is aware of what is expected of them may test the boundaries and try to over step them. In these cases quite often a simple look is sufficient to let them know that their behaviour is unacceptable. Eye contact should be used with the appropriate facial expression i.e. a look of disapproval.

Explanation of what will happen if the child persists in showing unwanted behaviour

Children should always be made aware of the consequences of their actions. Explaining the consequences underlines the importance of the rules and sets clear boundaries. Idle threats should never be made. If a child has been warned of a consequence and they continue to show unacceptable behaviour then it is paramount that the practitioner carries out the sanction they have imposed. Threatening sanctions that are unjustified or cannot be carried through will undermine the practitioner's authority and confuse the child.

Removal of the toy or equipment

This should always be used as a last resort. Children should be allowed to rectify their behaviour initially, through compromise and warnings, before the toy or equipment is removed. By removing a toy or equipment before giving the child the opportunity to rectify their behaviour they will have learned nothing. They will not know why the object has been taken away from them and they will probably move on to another toy and continue with the same unwanted behaviour. For example, if a child throws a toy across the room and is refused it back, they will usually proceed in picking up another toy and doing the same thing. A firm 'no' should be used initially, coupled with an expression of disapproval.

If the behaviour persists, and the child is old enough to understand, then an explanation should be given as to why it is not acceptable to throw toys indoors. For example, the toy may hit someone and cause injury, the toy may break something, or the toy itself may be damaged. When removing a toy or equipment from a child because they are displaying unacceptable behaviour and are refusing to cooperate, the practitioner should then find the child something else to do to prevent them from creating another inappropriate situation elsewhere. If appropriate, they could try offering the child the opportunity of going outdoors to throw a ball as an alternative to throwing a toy indoors.

Time out

Time out is *not* the same as isolation. Isolating a child is not an effective method of behaviour management, and practitioners should never put children into a room and leave them alone. If your practitioner is using this form of sanction question it immediately!

Time out is similar to removing toys and equipment in that it deprives the child of something they want. Time out allows both the child and the adult to calm down and take control of themselves. This method of behaviour management is particularly effective for more serious misdemeanours such as destructiveness, violence, swearing, rudeness etc. A few minutes 'time out' whereby the child is removed from the situation – taken to one side to calm down and reflect on their behaviour – should be all that is needed to diffuse the situation.

Time out is more appropriate for older children who will respond more effectively to being removed from a situation they are having difficulty with.

Time out should never be coupled with using a 'naughty chair' or 'naughty corner'. These are forms of humiliation and they will not help to calm a child down and may even encourage anger and resentment. Time out is not a punishment; it is a way of getting a child to calm down and to step back from the problem. Practitioners should offer reassurance and sympathy when talking to the child and will need to remember that emotions are very powerful and are often difficult for a child to control.

In addition to the above sanctions, some carers may feel the need to use punishments such as the 'naughty chair, step or corner'. How do you feel about this method of punishment? Is it something that you have tried successfully at home or do you think that it is over-rated and ineffective?

Professional childcare practitioners should never resort to humiliating a child as a method of punishment and placing them on a naughty chair is, in my opinion, a form of humiliation which should not be encouraged.

9

Understanding Contracts and Fees

If you are new to the world of childcare and have never had the experience of sourcing a suitable practitioner to care for your child then it is probably true to say that you may be finding the whole situation nerve-wracking and daunting. The task of sourcing and securing good quality childcare is in itself a mammoth feat, but add to this the pitfalls you may encounter regarding contracts, and you may wonder if it is all worth the hassle.

Contracts are in place to protect everyone and it is absolutely vital that you understand exactly what you are agreeing to before submitting your signature.

WHAT ARE YOU EXPECTED TO PROVIDE?

What you are expected to provide will depend very much on

the kind of service you and your child's carer have decided upon. The fees you pay may or may not include a number of things:

- meals, snacks and drinks;
- nappies and toiletries;
- playgroup fees;
- additional expenses such as the cost of outings and treats.

As a parent you will be expected to provide everything your child may require which is not included in the fee, for example nappies, toiletries and, in some cases even meals.

In addition you will also be requested to provide:

- a change of clothing for your child in the event of them soiling the clothes they arrive in;

- suitable clothing for outdoors, depending on the weather this may mean a warm/waterproof coat, wellingtons, hat and gloves;

- sun cream protection and a sun hat for summer months;

- medical products your child may require such as inhalers for asthma, teething gel etc.

The cost of food and drink is *usually* included in the fees charged by nurseries and some childminders. However others may charge additional amounts for meals or snacks, or insist that you provide your child's food yourself in the form of a packed lunch. You will need to discuss your child's requirements with the practitioner and decide on a suitable solution.

WHY IS IT NECESSARY TO HAVE A CONTRACT?

The simple answer to this question is so that all parties involved know exactly what is expected of them and where they stand. By law, all childminders and nursery settings must have a written contract with the parents or guardians of every child they look after. Contracts should be clear and concise and leave no room for misinterpretation. *Never* sign a contract unless you fully understand it and agree to the terms within.

This is an important checklist when considering contracts:

✓ Are you happy with the fee?
✓ What does the fee include?
✓ What are you expected to provide?
✓ Are the days and hours negotiated sufficient for your needs?
✓ Do you agree to the terms for sickness and holidays?
✓ Does the fee include bank holidays?
✓ Will you be expected to pay a deposit or retainer fee to secure your child's place?

HOW ARE YOU EXPECTED TO BEHAVE?

Respect cannot be demanded; it needs to be earned. You must always treat your child's carer politely and respectfully and, in turn, you should expect the same from them. Try to be as amicable as possible even if you feel things aren't to your satisfaction. It is always better to talk things through and reach a compromise before losing your temper and ending up having to find alternative childcare.

You will avoid confrontation and bad feeling if you keep your side of the bargain and try not to inconvenience your child's carer if at all possible. Expecting them to work overtime every day of the week will not get you off to a good start and will result in a bad atmosphere or even termination of contracts. Put yourself in the practitioner's shoes. How would you feel if your boss expected you to work extra hours every day, unpaid?

Good relationships

In order to ensure a good working relationship with your chosen practitioner always do the following.

■ **Stick to your contracted hours**. If you are going to be late due to unforeseen problems like traffic, be courteous and telephone your childminder/nursery and let them know of the delay. Be prepared to pay for the extra time you take.

■ **Pay on time**. No one wants to feel undervalued. If the practitioner is doing a good job then make sure they are paid on time according to your contract.

■ **Respect the rules of the setting**. These rules may differ from the ones you have at home but you must remember that they are in place to protect everyone present and you should assist the practitioner in implementing them at all times.

■ **Provide the necessary requisites** required for the practitioner to do their job satisfactorily. Nurseries may have nappies available for you to purchase should you forget to supply these, however is it really fair to expect a childminder to stock lots of different sizes?

■ **Do not expect the practitioner to care for your child if they are unwell**. Registration conditions clearly state that childcare providers should not care for a child with a contagious illness which may pose a risk to others. There is more about illness and back up cover in Chapter 7.

CONTRACTS AND WHAT THEY MEAN

What are contracts? A contract is an agreement between two parties. In the case of childcare this is between you, the parents, and your chosen practitioner. The contract is in place to make your and the practitioner's responsibilities clear. The contract is primarily about the care and well being of your child and it also sets out the obligations of both you and the practitioner. Always make sure that you have a contract. If you are not offered one, ask why and insist that this is rectified. All registered childcare practitioners should produce a legally binding contract setting out the terms and conditions of the childcare.

Reasons why you need a contract

- Contracts are designed to clearly set out the terms of the childcare arrangement.

- Contracts ensure that the business arrangement is kept on a professional level.

- Contracts can be personally tailored to meet the individual needs of each family and their circumstances.

- Contracts, once they have been signed and dated, are legally binding.

The kind of information which should be included in a contract

- The name, address and contact details of the practitioner, you and your child.

- The days and hours you will require your child to be cared for.

- The fees you will be charged.

- Date of payment and whether this should be paid on a weekly, monthly or termly basis and whether payment is due in advance or arrears.

- Details of fees payable during holidays – both your own and the practitioner's (in the case of a childminder/nanny).

- Details of fees payable in the case of sickness – both your child's and the practitioner's (in the case of a childminder/nanny).

- Details of who is responsible for playgroup fees, if this is appropriate.

- Details of charges incurred for late payment, early drop-offs or late collections. (If your nursery or childminder are good enough to waive these fees do not abuse their kindness by repeating the pattern regularly – everyone can be excused a late collection once in a while but when it happens two or three times a week do not be surprised if you are charged extra. This is, after all, overtime.)

- Details of the provisions you will be expected to bring such as suitable shoes and outdoor clothing, a change of clothes, nappies, formula milk, etc.

- Details of retainer fees and deposits.

- Amount of notice required for holidays and termination of contracts. Remember if the notice period for termination is four weeks and you only give one, you will be expected to pay the practitioner for the remaining three weeks, regardless of whether your child attends the setting or not.

▪ Review date.

If you are intending to employ a childcarer in your own home such as a nanny or an au pair then you may also like to add certain other clauses to the contract such as the following:

▪ Specific duties, other than caring for the child, that you expect them to carry out, such as laundry, light household chores, bathing children, etc.

▪ Details of tax and National Insurance payments.

▪ Details of any pension scheme that you are intending to provide.

▪ Details of disciplinary procedures. Outline sackable offences such as failure to carry out the duties adequately, incompetence, bad conduct etc.

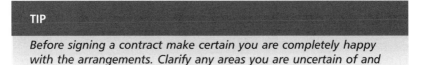

TIP

Before signing a contract make certain you are completely happy with the arrangements. Clarify any areas you are uncertain of and make sure your contract is reviewed regularly.

CHILDCARE FEES

Although some would say that the cost of childcare is unimportant, provided the service received is of the best quality, this is probably untrue in the majority of cases when parents are looking for suitable childcare. Of course emphasis is on the care provided and we all want the best for our children, however it is unwise to dismiss costs as irrelevant when, in many cases, they clearly aren't.

Value for money

Value for money is something that most of us look for and childcare is no exception. However, I have had enquiries from parents looking for childcare and my heart sinks when the first question they ask me is, 'How much do you charge?' Although I understand that cost is important, it would be nice to be asked about the service I provide and the experience and qualifications I have *prior* to enquiring about the fee.

Working parents are usually on a budget. Exactly how tight this budget is depends on the job they do and the circumstances they live by. Experience has taught me that it is not usually those on low incomes who barter about the cost. I have had high-fliers on hugely inflated incomes tell me that my fee of £2.70 per hour is unaffordable to them and much as they would love to enrol their child with me they can only do so if I reduce my prices!

HOW MUCH SHOULD I BE PAYING?

The cost of childcare varies immensely depending on the type of care you opt for and the area you live in. Childcare prices in London, for example, can often be twice as high as in areas in the North.

Childminders

You can expect to pay anything from £2.40 per hour to £4.00 per hour for a childminder. However, childminders in London may charge as much as £6.00 or £7.00 per hour. This rate can be much higher if you choose a childminder who is highly trained in a specialised area or who has gained a lot of qualifications and has a great deal of experience in their field. Concessions are sometimes made for families with more than one child in the setting but, although it is worth enquiring about reductions, do not assume these will be offered.

Nannies

Expect to pay between £130 per week to over £400 per week depending on the number of hours you require and how much experience the nanny has. The cost of employing a nanny varies considerably depending on the area you live in – again expect to pay higher rates in London – and whether you require the nanny to live in or out. In addition to these rates, you will also be expected to pay their tax and National Insurance contributions together with holiday and sick pay. Many nannies expect a mobile telephone to be provided, along with a car.

Nurseries

Once again, the cost of a nursery place will vary depending on where you live and you can expect to pay a much higher fee in London. Average weekly prices for a full-time nursery place for a child under the age of two years is about £130 rising to approximately £200 in London. Concessions are sometimes given to families who have two or more children in the setting although this is not always the case and good nurseries with a waiting list may not offer any reductions at all.

Extended schools

The cost of extended schools in your area will depend largely on whether there is any funding available. Prices can vary from £2–£3 for a place at a breakfast club to between £5 and £12 per day for an after school place.

The price you pay, for whichever form of childcare you choose, will depend largely on the area you live in, the age of your child and the number of days and hours you require. Expect to pay slightly more if you require a part-time place, particularly if the hours break into both morning and afternoon, for example 10am–2pm, as this will make it difficult for placements to be arranged around these hours. You may be expected to pay for a full day if the hours you require mean it is impossible to take on another child around them.

HOW DO I KNOW IF I AM PAYING TOO MUCH?

You will know if the fees requested are too high if you do your homework. Look around a number of childminders and nurseries and take into account the facilities on offer and the fees being charged. If the going rate for childminders in your area is £2.70 per hour but the one you particularly like charges £3.00 per hour, ask yourself why. Do they offer a better service? Is the menu more healthy and appealing? Does the fee include nappies, all meals and regular outings? If you cannot see clearly why the fee is higher, then ask the particular childminder.

There is no reason why you cannot mention to the childminder that, although you like the facilities they have to offer, you were wondering why the fees they charge are so much higher than the average rate for the area. Don't be aggressive, simply ask how the fees are set. If the childminder cannot give a valid reason and simply says that that is the fee she feels the service she provides deserves and is happy with the amount of business she is getting, then there is little you can do about it. Don't be fooled into thinking that, by mentioning that competitors in the area are charging less, you will get the childminder to lower her fees. If she has plenty of business and her existing customers are happy to pay the rate she asks, then she is unlikely to lower the fees for a new customer.

Reduced fees

Low or reduced fees are not always as appealing as they may first seem. A childminder charging 30p per hour less than her competitors may, at first glance, seem like a good deal but could actually work out more expensive when extras are added on. The childminder charging 30p extra may provide cooked meals included in the price or throw in nappies for free whereas the one charging the lower rate may request you to provide meals and nappies or charge extra for these, making the overall cost for comparison a much different story.

Qualifications and facilities

Finally, charges will vary considerably depending on the experience, qualifications and facilities the practitioner has to offer. For example, a childminder who runs her business from a fully equipped, self-contained play room designed completely around the children she cares for with an impressive array of toys and equipment, an outdoor play area, ten years' experience and a mountain of qualifications, is arguably in a better position to charge more for her service than a newly qualified childminder with little or no experience and only basic training running her business from the living room of her small house with no outdoor play area.

It is of course up to you, the parent, to decide exactly what you want for your child and how much you are willing to pay for it. Finances may dictate that you have to make compromises, however if this is the case, it should not mean a compromise on the quality of care rather the facilities and extras you receive.

IS THERE ANY FINANCIAL HELP AVAILABLE?

Before parents decide to go back to work after having children they often fall into the trap of thinking that good quality childcare is only for the well off and that they will be unable to afford it. Granted, for some parents, quality childcare takes up a large chunk of their annual salary but it is now more affordable to more people than ever before.

Whatever your own personal financial position there are many options for you to consider. Many benefits in the UK are not claimed by working parents as they either don't know they exist or they think they are not entitled to them. It is important that you thoroughly look into the benefits available as they can make a huge difference to the choices you have with regard to childcare.

The help available
- Child tax credit.
- Working tax credit.
- Childcare element of working tax credit.
- Employer supported childcare (otherwise known as the voucher scheme).
- Disabled child's premium.

Around 90 per cent of families are eligible for financial help with regard to childcare. Tax credits are awarded depending on your family circumstances and it is therefore important to inform the Tax Credit Office of any changes in your family's income.

Child tax credit

Usually families with a combined income of less than £58,000, or £66,000 if you have at least one child under the age of 12 months, will be eligible for this credit. The maximum amount of child tax credit a family can receive is around £33 per child per week. The credit is paid, in addition to child benefit, directly into the claimant's bank account and there are no work conditions on this benefit.

Working tax credit

Once again this credit is paid directly into your bank account and is aimed at people on low to middle incomes and can be used to help with childcare costs.

Childcare element of working tax credit

Extra help is available through the childcare element of the working tax credit and this is aimed at working parents to help them to cover some of the cost of their childcare. A maximum of 80p for every £1 you pay in childcare costs can be claimed, providing you use registered or approved childcare. There are limits to the amount of credit each family can claim and, at present, this stands at £175 per week for one child and £300 for two or more children per week. The childcare element of the working tax credit is paid directly to the child's main carer.

In order to be eligible to claim you must be either:

- a lone parent working a minimum of 16 hours per week;

- a couple who both work a minimum of 16 hours per week or whereby one partner works a minimum of 16 hours and the other is either incapacitated, in prison or in hospital.

To claim this benefit you must have a child in childcare who is either of school age or younger.

Employer supported childcare

More commonly known as the voucher scheme, this scheme is in addition to other tax credits and is offered to some employees by their employers to help pay for childcare. The scheme enables the employee to save on tax and National Insurance contributions on the first £55 per week of their salary which they use to pay for childcare. Providing you use a registered or approved form of childcare and your employer is part of a scheme, you can opt to have some of your wage paid by 'childcare vouchers' and make the tax and National Insurance contributions savings.

❝ *Payment by vouchers is both practical and easy* providing *parents remember to do their bit. The value of the voucher is paid directly into the carer's bank account eliminating the need to pay cheques or cash into the bank. However, if a parent forgets to hand over the voucher or go online to sort out payment, then the carer will have a long wait for their payment.*

Occasionally this has happened to me and it can be frustrating when parents forget to bring the voucher as it can take up to another five days for the money to be transferred into my account after the voucher has been redeemed. If you, the parent hand over the voucher a week late, your child's carer will have two weeks to wait for their money – so pay on time, every time. Vouchers are not cash and cannot be accessed immediately.

Disabled child's premium

If you are the parent of a disabled child you may be eligible to claim the disabled child element of the child tax credit. You will need to prove eligibility which can usually be done easily if you are also claiming the disability living allowance.

> **TIP**
>
> *Look at your finances carefully. Can you afford the childcare you want or will you have to compromise? Are you entitled to claim any of the benefits listed above? In addition to the fees charged are there any hidden extras such as trips and equipment for you to budget for?*

10

When Things Go Wrong

Unfortunately even the best laid plans can go wrong. Despite following all of the advice in this book, taking your time to source the right childcare, weighing up the pros and cons and thoroughly believing in the childcare provider you have chosen, you can still be let down. By following my advice you will definitely eliminate the majority of potential problems but, as with all things, nothing is foolproof and the potential to be let down is still a possibility. How you deal with any problems will be the deciding factor in whether or not you find yourself working things through with your existing provider or whether you end up looking for alternative childcare.

Depending on the nature of the problem and the extent of dissatisfaction you are feeling, you may decide to remove your child from the childcare setting and take matters further. I would advise all parents to try to resolve any issues with the practitioner before taking any drastic action unless you have serious doubts about the practitioner's capabilities.

DEALING WITH CONFLICT

Potential conflicts between parents and childcare providers can come about for a variety of reasons.

Reasons for conflict

- Either party may break the agreement or contractual arrangement. For example, you may fail to pay for the service or collect your child at the agreed time and the practitioner may fail to provide your child with the agreed cooked meal or take them to school on time.

- You may feel that the provider has breached confidentiality and spoken to others about you or your family's circumstances. Most breaches in confidentiality are a result of gossip and second-hand information. This can lead to a breakdown of trust between the two parties involved.

- Despite the arrangement working smoothly in the past, it may be that differences in attitudes to childcare begin to surface after a while and, whereas initially you may have been able to overlook problems, eventually the gap will widen and the situation is no longer acceptable to you.

- As your child grows and matures, problems, which may not have surfaced in the past, may become apparent, such as behaviour. You may disagree with the way your practitioner deals with unwanted behaviour for example, which in turn may lead to a disagreement between you both.

■ Poor communication may be at the root of a disagreement. You may be unclear what is expected of you and the practitioner may feel the same.

TIP

One of the most important things to remember in order to eliminate conflict is to communicate successfully. Be clear and concise and leave no doubt in the practitioner's mind exactly what you would like. Compromises may have to be made but only by letting the provider know your preferences can you be certain to have these taken into account. Poor communication often leads to misunderstanding.

MAKING A COMPLAINT

Complaints are stressful for everyone concerned. The person making the complaint may feel misunderstood and let down and the person receiving the complaint may be angry at being told that what they are doing is unacceptable. It is not usually the complaint alone that leads to resentment and anger, it is often the *way* in which the complaint is made that has the most effect.

Being angry, loud and bombastic will not help your case at all. If you have a complaint to make against a practitioner then do so in a calm and dignified manner. Put your message across without shouting or getting angry and allow the practitioner to explain their actions.

There is nothing more worrying than being unsure whether your child is being cared for properly and, in order for you to be happy, you need to be completely satisfied that the childcare your child is receiving is of good quality. It is probably true to say that parents worry more about the childcare their baby receives simply because their child is unable to tell them how they are feeling or what goes on in the childcare setting. Older children, who are capable of conversing, can often reassure us that they are happy in their daycare.

Procedures within the setting

Many daycare settings will have a written procedure for you to follow if you have any cause for complaint and you would be well advised to familiarise yourself with this procedure.

Ofsted is responsible for the registration and inspection of all voluntary, independent and local authority early years providers in England and all daycare providers and childminders must be registered with them. It is the job of Ofsted to evaluate the standard of care each provider offers and inspections are carried out periodically on each setting.

Unnecessary conflict

It is important to remember that everyone gets stressed from time to time. You will be tired after a busy day at work and you may be resentful at having had to sit in traffic for an hour. When you arrive at your child's nursery or childminding setting your child may not be ready to leave; they may be in the middle of an activity, eating their tea or engrossed in play. It is all too easy in this kind of situation to take your frustrations out on your child's carer. However this is a bad idea. They too may be tired after spending a stressful day caring for young demanding children and, if faced with a confrontational parent, this may be the final straw for them.

Try to look past niggles and irks which may have little or no consequence on the way your child is being cared for and may only be bothering you because you are tired. No one is perfect and, if your child is busy enjoying themselves should this be a cause for complaint just because you would have liked them to be waiting for you at the door with their coat on ready for a hasty retreat? It is the *real* problems which you need to know how to address.

WHEN YOU THINK YOUR CHILD ISN'T BEING CARED FOR PROPERLY

If you feel something is not right and you have doubts about the way your child is being cared for then you *must* say something. However it is often not *what* you say but *how* you say it that has the most effect. Ideally you will ask your child's carer if you can discuss the issue with them at a mutually convenient time. This may mean you coming back to the childminder's home later that evening or making an appointment to see the nursery manager. You should not expect to sort out any problems in front of the children while your child's carer is working. If possible there should be no children present when you discuss any issues and, most certainly no other parents, as the discussion should be completely private between the parties named in the childcare contract.

Just as it is important for the carer to be open, honest and approachable so too must you, the parent. It may well be that it is your child's carer who has an issue they would like to discuss with you. If you are unapproachable it makes sense that the carer will put off any discussion with you, perhaps until they can no longer cope, and then give you notice to end the contract rather than try to work things out and find a suitable solution for everyone concerned.

Tips for dealing with conflict or disagreements

If you have to raise an issue with your child's carer it is important that you always behave in the following ways.

- **Remain calm**. Never shout or raise your voice.

- **Remain friendly**. Never become aggressive or confrontational.

- **Be tactful**. Avoid being rude and remember if the issue you are raising is concerning something your child has told you they may well have got the wrong end of the stick! If you wade in with both feet without allowing the carer to explain anything you risk looking foolish if the information you have been given is incorrect or, in some cases, totally untrue.

- **Deal with one issue at a time**. If something has bothered you sufficiently to approach your child's carer with your concerns, deal with that particular issue. It is not necessary to back up your claims with other insignificant niggles and by doing so you risk deflecting from the nature of the original complaint and confusing your carer about exactly what issues you need addressing.

■ **Try to offer a solution to the problem yourself**. Tell the carer what you are unhappy about and offer suggestions for how things can be done differently which would be to your satisfaction. Be prepared that this may not be acceptable to your practitioner and make an effort to work together to find a compromise or solution.

■ **Remain positive**. If you give the impression that no solution can be found and that you are not willing to compromise you risk losing your child care arrangement altogether. Be positive, friendly and polite and be as amicable as possible.

Monitoring your child's progress

Once you have made a decision about the kind of childcare you would like for your child and you have settled them into the daily routine, it is absolutely vital that you continue to work with your child's carer every day. Your duty as a parent does not stop when your child is in daycare and you should remain actively involved in the childcare option you have chosen for your son or daughter.

It will be easier to keep track of things if your child is not a baby and he or she is able to talk to you and tell you about their day. It is highly unlikely that they will keep anything from you and, if they are unhappy about anything that has happened while they have been in daycare, your child is sure to tell you about it.

Although you may be concerned if your child is unhappy about something try to get things into perspective and, whenever possible, talk to your child's carer rather than fly off the handle and start making wild assumptions and accusations. Children can easily misunderstand comments and situations and quite often a simple, harmless remark can be made a dozen times worse if repeated by a distressed child.

Babies in childcare

If you have a baby in childcare then it will be all the more difficult for you to be completely certain that they are happy and settled in their environment as they will of course be unable to tell you about their day. Good communication with the carer is vital for this reason. Often a carer can reassure a doubting parent who constantly worries about her child, particularly if they cry when being left.

It is worth bearing in mind that there are other ways to reassure yourself that your child is being cared for well without the need for them to tell you.

Positive signs that your child is happy in daycare

■ Your child is happy to go to their carer.

■ Your child appears to mix well with the other children present.

■ Your child looks forward to spending time in the setting.

Negative signs that your child may not be being cared for adequately

■ Your child often seems to be crying when you collect them.

■ Your child often becomes distressed when you leave them (be careful when assessing this as many children who cry when their parents initially leave are happy and settled within minutes of their departure).

■ Your child is constantly tired when you collect them. This may be a sign that they are not being allowed adequate sleep during the day.

■ Your child appears to be hungry or thirsty all the time. This may be a sign that they are not being given adequate food and drinks.

■ Your child seems to develop nappy rash frequently. Unless there is an underlying reason for this, then frequent nappy rashes may be associated with inadequate nappy changing.

■ Your child has become clingy and withdrawn. If your child is usually happy and outgoing and their temperament changes drastically after starting daycare sessions then this may be a sign of poor-quality childcare.

HOW TO MAKE AN OFFICIAL COMPLAINT

I cannot stress enough how important it is to discuss any concerns you may have with the way your child is being cared for *initially* with your child's carer. Try, whenever possible, to talk things through with them, get to the root of the problem and find a solution. If this fails to result in a satisfactory outcome or if the concern you have is of a serious nature, then you will need to take the matter further and proceed through the official channels.

Many parents, whether for an easy life or through lack of information or courage, simply give their carer notice to terminate the contract, take their child out of the setting and find alternative childcare arrangements, when faced with a problem. However, although this may be the easy option for some parents, it is not the right thing to do. If you have a serious concern about the childcare your child is receiving, you have a duty to everyone involved to report your suspicions.

Steps to follow if you wish to make a complaint

■ Discuss your concerns initially with your provider. All daycare providers should have a complaints procedure for you to follow, setting out exactly what is required. Most concerns can be resolved at this stage and, unless you have a serious concern, it may be unnecessary for you to take things any further.

■ If you are not satisfied after following the settings procedure then contact the Ofsted Early Years Complaints Helpline on 0845 601 4772.

■ In the case of a serious complaint or if you think that your child or any other child in the setting may be at risk of abuse or neglect, then you should report your concerns immediately to the Ofsted Early Years Complaints Helpline on 0845 601 4772. In these cases it will also be necessary for you to inform your local authority's Child Protection Team (local numbers can be found in the telephone directory).

What happens next?

If you have cause for concern and feel that it is necessary to inform Ofsted of your suspicions, then it is a good idea to work out beforehand what you are going to say. Telephone the helpline number above and give as much accurate information as you can, noting the names of any key people involved, times and dates. Often you will be required to put your complaint in writing. Ofsted will inform you of exactly what will be required.

Many people prefer to make a complaint anonymously and, in many cases, it is possible for Ofsted to investigate complaints without having to reveal the complainants identity. Obviously, in some cases it may be possible for the provider to work out the identity of the complainant through the nature of the complaint, particularly if you have already approached the provider to try to sort things out beforehand and ended up removing your child from the setting. Ofsted cannot therefore guarantee anonymity, particularly if the investigation results in court proceedings.

Sometimes other professional agencies may need to be involved in the investigation, such as social services, but permission will be sought from the complainant before Ofsted pass on any details.

In exceptional cases such as those involving child protection then you must understand that Ofsted are obliged to pass on full details and information to both the police and social services in order for the necessary investigation to be carried out.

When the investigation is complete Ofsted will write to you. If the daycare provider gives their permission, you may be informed of the outcome of the investigation although this is not always possible.

COMPLIMENTS

Although most parents only involve Ofsted when they have a complaint to make, it is also possible for you to air your compliments. If you are particularly happy with the service your child has received, and many thousands of parents are, then tell your provider! Everyone works well when they are valued and appreciated and by sharing your pleasure with your child's provider you will be reassuring them of your appreciation and letting them know that you are happy with the work that they do. All too often we only notice the niggles and bad points and overlook the good. Ofsted are equally happy to hear your views and if you are particularly pleased with your childcare provider then let Ofsted know by telephoning the Early Years Helpline on 0845 601 4771.

When carrying out inspections of settings Ofsted try, whenever possible, to speak to parents using the service and some providers ask parents to complete a questionnaire so that they can share their views and opinions with the inspector. If your provider asks you to complete a questionnaire try to be as honest as possible backing your comments up, wherever possible, with examples of the good service your practitioner has provided.

11

Questions to Ask

Finding the right childcare for your family's needs is no easy task. Although there are many providers offering an array of services, tracking down and securing a place with someone, who not only shares your own parenting views and opinions but also gets on well with your children, is probably one of the hardest tasks you will ever have to do.

You may be very lucky finding the right childcare solution first time and staying with them throughout your child's early years or you may stumble across problems and end up having to change your childcare arrangements.

One thing is for sure, the more effort you put in initially the more likely you are to find suitable childcare early on. Do your homework, shop around, make enquiries and be choosy! There are a lot of providers to pick from and not all providers are good at their job. Just because someone works in the field of childcare and has a relevant qualification doesn't mean that they are good at their job or that they are the best person to care for your child.

As with all professions some childcare workers will be better at their job than others, some will be more committed and dedicated than others. To help you to make the right decision you would be advised to read this book thoroughly and then ask as many questions as possible and request as many details and as much information as you can before making any final decisions.

QUESTIONS TO ASK WHEN MAKING TELEPHONE ENQUIRIES

- What is the exact location of the childcare premises?

- What hours is the childcare facility open?

- Are there are any vacancies?

- Is the facility open all year round or does it close for holidays; if it closes how many weeks does it close for?

- Is there a back up service in place to cover closures for holidays and illness?

- How many children does the facility currently cater for?

- What are the ages of the children currently enrolled in the facility?

- Does the facility cater for part-time hours?

- Do the staff hold any childcare qualifications?

■ Are the staff trained in first aid?

If the answers to these questions meet with your approval and the provider has a vacancy, then it is a good idea to make an appointment to visit the facility. If the provider appears suitable but has no vacancies at present, then enquire about the possibility of being placed on the waiting list and request that they contact you should a vacancy arise in the near future.

QUESTIONS TO ASK A PROSPECTIVE NANNY

■ What made you decide to become a nanny?

■ What experience have you got in working as a nanny?

■ Who was your most recent employment with?

■ What were your duties during your last employment?

■ Why did you leave your last employment?

■ What kind of training do you have?

■ Do you hold any recognised qualifications such as NNEB?

■ Are you trained in first aid?

■ What ages of children do you have the most experience in working with?

■ Are you willing to make a commitment to the family of say a minimum of twelve months?

■ What salary are you expecting?

■ Are you willing to do any light household duties?

- Do you drive? If so, do you own a car?

- What days and hours are you available to work?

- What holiday entitlement do you expect?

- Have you got any holidays booked?

- When are you available to start work?

- Do you have any references?

- Would you be willing to undertake a medical examination and background check prior to commencing work?

QUESTIONS TO ASK WHEN CONSIDERING A DAY NURSERY

- Do you have a copy of your latest Ofsted report available for inspection?

- How many children are you registered to care for?

- What ages of children do you provide care for?

- How many members of staff are there and what ratios of adults to children do you have?

- What policies and procedures does the setting have in place with regard to:
  - behaviour management;
  - confidentiality;
  - equal opportunities;
  - safety;
  - collection of children.

- What kind of activities do you provide?

- Do you arrange outings for the children?

- Is there a secure outdoor play area?

- What kind of meals do you provide? Do you have any sample menus?

- What is the nursery's usual daily routine?

- Are all the staff fully trained? What qualifications do they hold?

- Are all the staff trained in first aid?

- How does the nursery work in partnership with parents?

- How does the nursery support children who are potty training?

- What is the settings policy for sick children?

- Who would be assigned to work with your particular child and what is their background and experience?

- What fees does the facility charge?

- Do you have any vacancies?

- Do you take children on a part-time basis?

QUESTIONS TO ASK A PROSPECTIVE CHILDMINDER

- Do you have a copy of your latest Ofsted report available?

- How many children are you registered to care for?

- How many children are you currently caring for?

- What are the ages of the children that you are currently providing care for?

- What is your usual daily routine?

- Do you take children on a part-time basis?

- Have you got any vacancies?

- Which schools, nurseries and playgroups do you service?

- Do you attend toddler groups and support groups?

- Do you take children to the library?

- Do you arrange outings? If so, where to?

- Do you encourage children to become a part of your local community?

- What activities do you provide?

- Where is your childminding service run from?

- What facilities do you have for example, a separate playroom or outdoor area?

- How much experience do you have in caring for children and at what ages?

- Do you have any childcare qualifications?

- Are you trained in first aid?

- What kind of meals and snacks do you provide?

- Do you have any written policies?

■ What is your policy for behaviour and discipline?

■ Do you have any children of your own, if so how many and of what ages? Remember childminders must count any children of their own in their registration numbers.

■ Do you have any pets? If so, what kind and will the children have access to them?

DO'S AND DON'TS WHEN CHOOSING AND ARRANGING CHILDCARE

Do

✓ Do look at all the options available. Make a note of your requirements and contact your local Children's Information Service (CIS) for details of the childcare available in your area.

✓ Do shop around. *Never* settle for the first setting you look at. You will need to look at several settings before being able to compare the facilities on offer.

✓ Do consider your child when making any decisions. Your child's age and personality is likely to have a huge impact on the kind of childcare you choose.

✓ Do follow up references.

✓ Do ask around for opinions. Usually the best people to talk to are other parents using the facilities. Find out what they particularly like or dislike and see whether this has any affect on your own considerations.

✓ Do sign a contract which states exactly what has been agreed so that everything is official.

✓ Do visit the setting more than once to be absolutely sure that you are happy with the arrangement.

Don't

✗ Don't leave things until the last minute. Give yourself plenty of time to shop around and choose the best childcare for your child.

✗ Don't rule out mixing your childcare arrangements if your preferred choice isn't available to accommodate all the days you need. Combining childcare, for example, three days with a childminder and two days with a nursery can often work very well and you will be in a good position to take advantage of vacancies as soon as they become available.

✗ Don't feel guilty about leaving your child.

✗ Don't feel guilty about taking up references and double-checking arrangements.

Useful Websites

Association of Nanny Agencies (ANA) www.anauk.org

British High Commission/Home Office (au pair scheme) www.britishhighcommission.gov.uk

Care Standards Inspectorate for Wales (CSIW) www.csiw.wales.gov.uk

Care to Learn – for information regarding finances and flexible working www.dfes.gov.uk/caretolearn

Childcare Approval Scheme www.childcareapprovalscheme.co.uk

ChildcareLink www.childcarelink.gov.uk

Disability Rights Commission – for information regarding care for children with special needs www.drc-gb.org

Disclosure Service (The Criminal Records Bureau) www.crb.gov.uk

Equal Opportunities Commission www.eoc.org.uk

International Nanny Association www.nanny.org

National Association of Family Information Services (NAFIS) www.nafis.org.uk

National Childminding Association (NCMA) www.ncma.org.uk

National Day Nurseries Association www.ndna.org.uk

Northern Ireland Childminding Association www.nicma.org

Office for Standards in Education (Ofsted) www.ofsted.gov.uk

Scottish Childminding Association www.childminding.org

Scottish Commission for the Regulation of Care (SCRC) www.carecommission.com

Sure Start www.surestart.gov.uk

Working families helpline – for information regarding finances www.working families.org.uk

Index